A GATHERING OF WAYS

Also by John Matthias

Poetry
Bucyrus 1970
Turns 1975
Crossing 1979
Bathory & Lermontov 1980
Northern Summer 1984

Translations
Contemporary Swedish Poetry 1980
(with Göran Printz-Påhlson)

Jan Östergren: Rainmaker 1983
(with Göran Printz-Påhlson)

The Battle of Kosovo 1987
(with Vladeta Vučković)

Editions
23 Modern British Poets 1971
Introducing David Jones 1980
David Jones: Man and Poet 1989

A GATHERING OF WAYS

JOHN MATTHIAS

*For Bernie
— on his retirement
from Notre Dame
w/ all best wishes
from John and Diana
May 8, 1994*

SWALLOW PRESS/
OHIO UNIVERSITY PRESS
ATHENS

A Gathering of Ways is made possible in part by support from the Institute for Scholarship in the Liberal Arts, College of Arts and Letters, University of Notre Dame. The author also acknowledges support from the Ingram Merrill Foundation.

Swallow Press/Ohio University Press books are printed on acid-free paper. ∞

Library of Congress Cataloging-in-Publication Data

Matthias, John, 1941-
   A gathering of ways / John Matthias.
     p. cm.
   ISBN 0-8040-0941-4. — ISBN 0-8040-0945-7 (pbk.)
   I. Title.
PS3563.A858G38   1991
811'.54 — dc20   90-20684
                                           CIP

96   95   94   93   92   91   5   4   3   2   1

ACKNOWLEDGEMENTS

"An East Anglian Diptych" was first published in *Poetry Wales*, Vol. 21, No. 2, and then in *Another Chicago Magazine*, No. 15. "Facts From an Apocryphal Midwest" was excerpted in *Prospice*, No 26, and published complete in *Another Chicago Magazine*, No. 17. Three sections from "A Compostela Diptych" were published in *TriQuarterly*, No. 76. Grateful acknowledgement is made to the editors of these journals.

An East Anglian Diptych:
Ley Lines, Rivers

In Memoriam
Robert Duncan and David Jones

Ley Lines

i.

...& flint by salt by clay
by sunrise and by sunset
and at equinox, by equinox,

these routes, these
lines were drawn, are drawn,
(force by source of sun)

The dowser leans by Dod-man's
ley alignment and
against some oak by water now.

ii.

By flint: the tools
By salt: the meats
By clay: the rounded pots

Along the lines, by sun-
rise & by sunset
and at equinox, by equinox,

the Dod-man's sighting staves,
one in each hand, is it,
of that scoured long chalk man?

iii.

Past Tom Paine's house behind the puddingstone
and castle there aligned
strategically along the Icknield way

Beyond the Gallows Hill
beside the Thetford tracks to Brandon
down the Harling Drove

Across the Brickkiln Farm to Bromehill Cottage
& below the tumuli before
the rabbit warrens and top hats...

Some burials, some dead,
and here their flinted offerings.
Seven antler picks,

A phallus made of chalk,
a Venus (did they call her yet Epona?)
and a tallow lamp...

Beltane fire line forty miles long?
Conflagration's law where energy's electric
down the *herepath*

if *Belus* is spelt *Bel*...

•

No bronze until the Beakers.
No phosphorus lucifers until, say, 1832.
Toe holes, ropes allowed descent

for wall stone you could antler out,
shovel with a shoulder bone—
Floor stone you would crawl for...

Between the galleries, burrows
narrow as a birth canal, as dark,
where some half-blinded Neolith first

nudged the Brandon Blacks & passed
those flints as far down time as Waterloo.
Weapons, tools. Ornaments as well.

Flushwork on Long Melford Church.
Flint flake Galleting on Norfolk Guildhall.
Jags by thousands of the calcined stones

for Queen Victoria's potteries.
Strike-a-lights required on Maundy Thursday still—
oldest flints ignite a young god's Pascal wick,

But first an edge to cut away the underbrush
down ley lines
long before the Beakers and their bronze.

iv.

Ten days, twelve chapters, and the young man soon to
die at Arras finishes his book, his thirtieth or so, on the
Icknield way. It's mostly about walking. He walks from
Thetford where he thinks the Way begins coming from
the Norfolk ports across the River Thet and Little
Ouse. He's melancholy. The times are difficult, he's
poor, he'd rather be a poet, his wife is desperate for his
company, his children miss him too, a war is coming on,
and, anyway, he's melancholy by nature. He has a
friend who tries to show him how to turn his prose to
verse. He'll have two years to do just that before he dies
on Easter Monday, 1917.

But now he walks and writes. It is a job. They pay you
for these nature books, these evocations, all this nam-
ing you can do along the road and through the villages
and over all the dykes. They'll buy your eye even if

they're deaf to all this balancing of consonants and vow-
els. He's melancholy. He doesn't really want to take this
walk. He does it for the money. The times are difficult,
he's poor, he'd rather be a poet, his wife is desperate for
his company, his children miss him too, a war is coming
on. Still,

It's better on a path than on a pavement.
It's better on the road than in a town.
It's better all alone to walk off melancholy
than to poison a companionable air
(or stare out of a muddy trench in France.)

Home, returned on leave, exhausted,
bored by prose he's published only months before
and talking with a friend who'll ask:
And what are you fighting for over there?

he'll pick a pinch of earth up off the path
they're walking and say: *This!*
For this, he'll say.
This This This
For
        this

        •

This King Belinus was especially careful
to proclaim that cities
and the highways that led unto them

would have the peace
Dunwello had established in his time.
But no one seemed to know

the rules or lines whereby the boundaries
of the roads had been determined.
Neither Geoffrey, who, saying that about

Belinus in his book then consults the works
of Gildas, nor Gildas either,
nor Nennius himself in *Historia Brittonum.*

Before Belinus paved the road to "Hamo's Port"
with stone and mortar as he paved
Foss Way and Watling Street, walkers who

brought flint, brought salt, brought clay,
paved the way in footprints over peat
and grasses with their animals before them

or behind. *By flint:* the tools;
By salt: the meats; *by clay:* the rounded pots.
By ley lines, flint and clay and salt

by sunrise and by sunset
and at equinox, by equinox, these routes,
these lines were drawn

(but no one seemed to know the rules
whereby the boundaries
of the roads had been determined)

force by source of sun.

v.

They leaned into the journey,
east to west,
beyond Grimes Graves and through

the place that would be Thetford.
For every dragon heard to have been slain,
they found a standing stone....

Beside the Hill of Helith and then
along the river Lark
they left their weapons and their coins,

wondered at the headless rider
riding on the muddy banks. Cautious, curious
at the Swales tumulus, at

barrows north of Chippenham, they guessed
fine Wessex bronze lay gleaming
in the buried dagger there...and aged (grew young),

passed by Burwell church, passed by
Burwell castle too, spoke
of Anna and of Etheldreda, queen and saint,

at Exing, saw the horses race along
by Devil's Ditch to Reach, gallop through
the sainfoin which they gathered

in their hands as stone aligned with stone,
church with church, holy well
with holy well, pylon (in the end) with pylon.

Counting *one five four: four seven four:*
four eight six at Whittlesford,
brides among them turned their heads

to gaze at Golliwog, Shiela-na-gig.
Whose giggle, then, this
gog-eyed goggle goddess ogling back

above the portal near the Wandlebury
Gogmagog? *By air:* the zodiac;
By fire: the dragon path; *by earth:*

the tumulus, the barrow and the grave.
East to west
they leaned into the journey where

the dowser leans by Dod-man's
ley alignment and
against some oak by water now.

Rivers

i.

By touch: his twig reveals the waters,
his sounding rod bites into chalk.
Matrona, Bel and Wandil gather in the mist

upon the hillside, lean into the journey:
moon by sun against the darkness,
sun by moon against the giant with a sword.

By air: the signal from the Gogmagogs
to zodiacs at Edmund's Bury and Nuthamstead.
Knight to knight come forth. By air

the still response: the bull, the lion;
the eagle & the bear. If Wandil stole the spring,
spread his frost along the ley lines,

now he strides as Gemini across the sky.
(Not two children, not two goats,
but eyes of Wandil rain down geminids

where ancient Dod-men lie....)

ii.

By water now. Along the Lark to Bury
where by air the constellations
blaze down on these figures born of earth.

Was it before Beodricsworth became
Saint Edmund's town & shrine
that Sigebert's forebears paced off zodiacs

from Abbots Bridge to Stoke-by-Clare
discerned as fit propitiation still
by him who led the garlanded white bull

to its oblation for the barren girl
between imposing portals
of the Benedictine Abbey on the Lark?

By rivers then. Along this quiet one
past Bury where it forms
the tail of Sagittarius and on by sting

of Scorpio, by tribute and by tributary,
portaging on over Virgo
north of Shimpling to Chad Brook....

Where the Stour flows by Long Melford
they leaned into their journey, rowed along
the belly of the Lion close by Clare.

If Wandil gestured to the west, they
travelled east toward Harwich, backs against
the morning sun, oars against the tide.

Underbrush along the banks at first
held only otters, then at Mysteleigh solemn men
sat fishing, men knelt making salt;

at Manningtree, a single lighter hauled
the heavy stones up shallow higher reaches
where a mason waited with his tools

and visions of a chancel in his brain.
Stoke and Wilford built their low stone bridges then;
other towns built locks; local wool

brought bricks and lime and coal.
West to east, they met the horse-drawn barges,
passed young woodsmen felling trees

to build the *Thorn*, the *Syren* and the *Terpsichore*.
Lark by Stour by Orwell; Scorpio
by Lion. Moon by sun against the darkness.

Sun by moon. A giant with a sword....

iii.

Or with a ship. A *Syren* or a *Terpsichore*. And if a giant,
then a giant metamorphosed over time. The man
who'll six years later paint the *Hay Wain* may not know
his river rises as a tiny brook east of the Chilterns in the
Gogmagogs. And yet he feels the giant in it, yet he
knows its gods. Today he finishes his sketch of Flatford
Mill—the mill itself, the locks, the barge and bargemen,
and the small distracted barefoot boy on his horse. He'll
work it up in 1817 for the Academy and no one will
complain that it lacks finish. The sketch itself is rough.
He adds an ash—his favorite tree—some elms, a bro-
ken oak. He shades in clouds he's come to study with a
meteorologist's precision. Then he shuts the sketch
book and trudges off toward Dedham, marking in his
mind the river's fringe of willowherb and reed, the ris-
ing heron and the darting snipe and redshank in the
sky...

He wants to marry Charles Bicknell's daughter. He
wants to paint this river and these shimmering green
fields. He doesn't want to quarrel with Charles Bick-
nell, with the rector of his village, or with Bonaparte.

And he doesn't want to paint for money portraits of the
rich or of their homes: Malvern Hall, Petworth House,
East Bergholt. The ships that followed *Thorn* on down
the slips at Mistly shipyards belched a thousand years of
Beltane fire at French sails on the Nile. Martello towers
rose at Shotley and at Walton Ferry...But here and now
it's quiet, he thinks. Here and now it's peaceful and the
air is pure...

It's better to paint rivers than great houses.
It's better to be married than alone.
It's better with companionship to sit through winter nights
remembering the Stour in springtime
(or a cousin lying face-down in the mud at Waterloo).

Here, returned from London, nervous and annoyed,
bored by portraits that he's painted only months before
and talking to a friend who asks:
And what are you drawing landscapes for out here?

he picks a pinch of earth up off the path
they're walking and says *This!*
For this, he says.
This This This
For

      this

    •

This other ryver called of old time
Fromus maketh his beginning
near to Framlingham and then descendeth

close by Marlesford and so
southeast of Farnham entertayneth yet
another ryver called the Gleme

which cometh out from Rendlesham
thus passing forth to Snapebridge and
contriving then his course to Yken

dedicates himself into the sea
not very far away from where the Stour & Orwell
run together into Harwich harbour.

Framlingham: Framela's people: strangers on
the Fromus before Fromus became Alde.
Folk who'd become burgen-holders paying 5d tax.

On the bluff above the mere the Bigods' castle
glowers: Henry's castle glowers back
from Orford. Herrings, cereals, pottery from

Staverton passed through the town, began a journey
inland or a journey to the coast.
Scratchings on the nave in Parham church

show navigable reaches: ships of little draft
came all the way from Normandy past
Orford, Sloughden, Iken, down this stream

that flows
into a pipe below a petrol station

      now

iv.

...Men will number
what they value most
in wills: 'To Robert Cook my scalbote,

my anchor and the things belonging to it and
my spurling bote: to George Clare
my fysher, fartle, makerel nets & warropes:

To John Weylonde: A manfare of haryngnetts:
capstaynes, skewers & my sparlyng netts
that hangeth in the low to the sea this yere

and when the sparlyngfare is done the netts
schal then be partyd to my children:
Thomas, Christopher, Erasmus: ships belonging

to the havyn to be sold at Aldeburgh church.'
The men who made the wills were fishermen;
The others built their boats along these shores...

or sold them victuals, or worked upon the land,
or herded sheep, kept inns, cut
the timber, prayed in church & monastery, wept

impressed at sea, took up piracy and smuggling,
made the malt that made the ale they drank,
organized themselves in unions, and were hanged.

By 1850 photographs appear to show us
what they looked like outside Newton Garrett's
maltings or beside their barges loading

at Snape quay. John Felgate, shipwright, has
no teeth and wears a cap of moleskins;
his son, standing by a dinghy, has a thick

mustache, a threadbare coat, & a determined gaze.
Jack Ward, skipper of the *Gladys,* smiles;
his heavy begrimed turtleneck presses up against

his graying whiskers and his wide square chin.
The carpenters, Alfred Andrews & his son,
look almost well-to-do beside the shipwrights;

the younger Andrews wears a tie, a waistcoat,
and a golden chain while sawing timber for a rudder
or a boom; Howell and Chatten, maltsters,

hold their massive wooden shovels, handles down,
and slop about in canvas boots. Their rugged faces
look like copper pennies in a winter sun.

If we could hear them speak we'd doubtless hear
them say how *chance-times a sloe-wind*
brings old Tabbler Cable back to that same mawther

who'd 'im clapper-clawed or hear them laugh about
the crones who *couldn't sculpt the roots*
out as they got no teeth. The carter thakketh his hors

upon the croupe and jumps up in his wagon.
He's off to town. The men who work the maltings
and the bargemen line up for their pay.

The bird that flies above them angling toward
the Orford Ness they call a *mavis;*
by the time it reaches sprawling spider-webs

of early-warning radar nets it's lost its name,
and anyone at Chantry Point
looking with binoculars for avocets or curlews

would only see, if it passed by, a thrush.
Along the ley-alignment point
at Sizewell, Beltane fires in the reactor

are contained by water drained out of the sea.

v.

　　　...But that the salt sea of say AD 500
should be drained from Deben marshes
that the land be sweet for corn and cattle...

That the river rising beyond Sutton, beyond
Woodbridge wait out flood & tide
for Norman engineers and then the Dutch,

for every local Fosdike, every local Waller
who might learn the warping
and the inning, reclaim with bank & seawall

or with sluice & gutter marshes then defended
by the reeves of Walton and
the men of Melton who might write: *lately salt,*

now fresh... That would take some time.
Some time, too, before the signals flash from
castle cresset, lucomb, lighthouse

or Martello tower up and down the coast
from Goseford to the Alde. No
early warnings here where everything's surprise.

South to north, they leaned into the journey,
rounded Landguard Point and
passed by Walton Castle, sailing with the tide

across the sand bar, steersman hugging
his athwartship tiller, small rain
in the oarsmen's eyes, wind across the stern.

Beyond the sandy heathland, the turf & bracken
over which they'd lug a ship the
size of this one to be buried as a cenotaph—

with coins from Usson-du-Poitou, a golden helmet,
maple lyre, & stone sceptre carved
with eight stern faces and a thin bronze stag

mounted on its delicate iron ring—
they reached the pools they sought and, anchoring
off mud flats, felled the trees,

built their timber halls beyond abandoned villas,
stayed at Hemley, Hatchley, Trimley,
called the river that they sailed "the deep one."

They'd say they lived in *Middanyeard,* where *haeleth
under heofenum:* they found themselves
between two seas... (the hero of their poem the sun).

Before them, Celts and Roman legions.
After them the Viking raids.
After them the Norman engineers and Flemish traders.

Before them, the single salters squatting
on the mud, the long walk for flints
along the Icknield way. After them the excavation

of the buried ship....

●

Extensio. Eastern point
north of Southwold on the Easton Ness, now lost.
Portus Adurni. Was the Deben called Adurnus

by the Latins here and on the Alde?
Harbour, temperate climate, sheltered creeks—
and vines growing high above the cliffs.

Counts of the Saxon Shore constructed here
their fortress where they failed to hold the tide
against the kin of those first called

by Vortigern to fight his wars against the Picts.
(St. Alban's first cartographer
would clearly mark his map: *Angulus Anglie...*)

Around the corner, then, and up the river
with the driftwood & the tide. Buoyed and beaconed,
spits and banks first marked with small

bouquets of yellow broom display their
angled emblems: Bowships beacon, Middleground,
Upper Waldringfield and Lower Ham,

Jack Rush beacon, Crimmy Moore, Horse Buoy.
If Edward were to anchor here
along the Kingsfleet, who but the Archbishop

might come sailing smartly out of Shotley
as the king, shining like some Helith, went to meet him
round into the Stour? On board the *Thomas,*

19

in a western wind, the Goseford ships impressed
for service, the power upon them
& Calais in fear, they'd break up the Great Seal.

So Wandil on the Stour gestures gravely
to the Wandil on the Gogmagogs. Against him lean
the sun & moon while all about him

widdershins there turns a circle of the dancers
who will help achieve the spring
as every ley south-east of Thetford Castle Mound

lines up along the tumuli and standing stones
to pass through places named for Bel
or Belus out to Walton on the northern Sea....

Beyond the Roman camp, the Saxon mound.
Beyond the Saxon mound the Viking
outpost in the Celtic forest with its secret paths.

Along the paths, the route to tributaries,
creeks, the sweetest hidden wells. Above the wells
a dowser with his twig, a Dod-man

with his sighting staves....

•

who walks along the concrete wall,
and feels the fresh salt air,
and watches small yachts ply the quiet river

at high tide. Red sails, blue.
And bright white hulls. Woodbridge Sunday sailors
tack and jibe...

Alde by Stour by Deben. Ship by Saxon shore.
Cattle, corn by sea wall.
Dod-man, dowser, dapple of reflected cloud.

Facts From an Apocryphal Midwest

For Ken Smith and Michael Anania

1. Seven Moves Toward Embarcation on the Local River

Nous embarquâmes le troisième Decembre
avec trente hommes, dans huit canots

& nous remontâmes la rivière des Miamis
faisant nostre route au Sud...

—Fr. Hennepin

•

Overheard on Riverside cycling toward
the bridge and U.S. 31:
Look, he says, *if things had turned out*

differently a long time back,
not just you, but everybody on this
river might be speaking French

& trading otter skins or beaver pelts.

•

1 arpent: 160 *pieds de Roi*
84 arpents: say about one league
28 arpents, then, to the mile

But distances are tricky
and it often takes
you longer
than you think.

•

Four thin men, two white, two black
stand fishing near the Farmer's Market
where the Amish come to sell

their vegetables and breads. It's early
afternoon in heavy, muggy August.
The river's low & stagnant for ten miles.

Catchin' anything? Jus' tin cans an' tires
Four thin fishermen—
and no Miamis, not a Potawatomi in town.

●

Oui-oui-la-Meche
L'Espérance de la Brie

Père Gabriel
Père Louis
Père Zénobe

Réné Robert Cavelier (Sieur de la Salle)

●

"There were several varieties of league; but the
one that Hennepin undoubtedly meant was the ordi-
nary league of 84 arpents. That will give 3.051 plus
5220-5280th statute miles. You need have no hesita-
tion in assuming Hennepin's league to be 3.052 statute
or English miles."

"We embarked on the 3rd of December with
thirty men in eight canoes, and ascended the river of
the Miamis, taking our course to the south-east for
about twenty five leagues. We could not make out the

portage which we were to take with our canoes and all
our equipage in order to go and embark at the source of
the river Seignelay, and as we had gone higher up in a
canoe without discovering the place where we were to
march by land to take the other river which runs by the
Illinois, we halted to wait for the Sieur de La Salle, who
had gone exploring on land; and as he did not return
we did not know what course to pursue."

—Fr. Hennepin

2. Five Maps, a Medicine Bag, and a Myth

•

Carte de la Nouvelle Découverte

Illuminations of the priests haranguing Indians.
Much conjecture. Crudely drawn Ohio
and Missouri and Wisconsin...
Père Marquette's route back it's got
entirely wrong.

•

Carte Généralle de la France Septentrionale

The Ohio's called the *Ouaboustikou*.
Pictures of the creatures
native to the Mississippi's western plains
include a camel, ostriches, giraffes.
A monster seen by Père Marquette and Joliet:

Horns of a deer, beard of a tiger,
face like that of a man—Also
many nasty scales
and a long tail wound around it.

•

Carte de Jean Baptiste Franquelin

La Salle's Starved Rock, a natural fortress
all but inaccessible a hundred feet
above the Illinois, the little colony below.
La Nouvelle France: Penobscot
to the south of Lake Champlain and to
the Mohawk near Schenectady
and then where Susquehanna rises
and the Allegheny past the south of Erie
on to Southern Michigan & then
northwest to Mississippi tributaries.
La Louisiane: The Mississippi valley,
the Ohio valley, Texas.
Rivière Colbert. Grande Rivière des Emissourittes.
Rivière des Illinois, ou Macopins.
And down below Starved Rock the colony:
Shawnees, Ouiatenons, Miamis,
Piankishaws, Illinois, Kilaticas, & Ouabonas.
3,900 warriors huddling
under *Le Rocher* & trembling for the Iroquois.

•

Carte de M. Mathieu Sâgean

The nation of the Acanibas, towns and castles,
King Hagaren, Montezuma's kin.
Women riding unicorns. Bricks of solid gold.
Caravans of horsemen
and a thousand oxen bearing priceless treasures.
Everyone polygamist.
Perpetual summer there, a cool breeze.

●

Rand McNally Atlas, 1985

The old Sauk trail, they say
still runs under U. S. 12
north from Niles to Detroit.
U.S. 20 takes it west through
Rolling Prairie to Chicago.

You can drive a car that's named
for Cadillac up U. S. 12
to Ypsilanti, turning north
at 94 to a port named for the Hurons.
You can even drive
your Pontiac to Pontiac.
But only trickster Wiske's brother
Chibyabos ever drove
in a Tecumseh to Tecumseh.

●

What's in your medicine bag, Neshnabe?
Gifts from Wiske? Toys?

A skunk's bladder. Ear of a bat.
Three fat joints and a switchblade knife.
Pussy hairs from Mama Chickie's whores.
What's in your map, little Frog?
If I drop this at your feet, it will explode.

•

The story goes that poor and feeble Tisha had a vision. A stranger dressed elaborately in clothing he had never seen before appeared and said he'd build a boat for him to travel over land and sea and rivers in if Tisha showed him just how big it ought to be. Tisha then took twelve enormous paces, smiled at the solemn stranger, waited. Suddenly a ship appeared the likes of which he'd never seen or even dreamed of. It had thin tree trunks planted vertically upon its decks, it had white sheets attached, it had nine great black guns. Boat-Maker and Tisha climbed aboard and sailed over land and sea and rivers. They met and took aboard a mighty seer, a mighty hearer, a mighty eater, a mighty runner, and a mighty maker of wind. These were Boat-Maker's friends.

One day after many travels they arrived at the camp of evil Matjimanito. He and all his friends were cannibals, and many bones lay all around. Matjimanito challenged Tisha to a contest where he'd gamble for his life. When Boat-Maker saw poor Tisha trembling, he insisted on a game which Matjimanito had never played before. When Tisha shouted *now*, Wind-Maker blew the ship up in the air above the village shouting out: *everybody's bones get out of here!* The nine black cannons fired, the dead all came alive, and Matjimanito and his men all perished when the ship came down and crushed them. After that, Tisha was a famous man. He

travelled all the world over with his elegant protector
and his friend. Eventually, Boat-Maker taught him
how to speak his language. It was French.

3. Copper. South from Lake Superior

...and down the old Sauk trail
although there were then, three and more millennia
before the French, no Sauks....

The trail itself was there, and those who mined
the copper, *they* were there,
and those who came on urgent journeys from

the lower Mississippi & the Gulf to lug it back
were there, and leaned into
their labors in the mines and on the paths.

Mounds at Moorhouse Parish, at Miamisburg,
tumuli along the northeast
of the marshy lake between the Kankakee and

Portage Prairie with its recent graves & glacial
memories of mastodon & mammoth spit up
needles, chisels, knives & awls in fine profusion—

& when Bernal Diaz entered Tuspan with Cortez,
he found that *every Indian had,*
besides his ornaments of gold, a copper axe,

very highly polished, strangely carved.
The copper came from west and north
of Mackinaw, Sault Ste. Marie, & Whitefish point,

from Minong where ten thousand men once mined
the copper for a thousand years
but left no carvings, writings, signs, nothing

but their simple tools. Their dead they
buried elsewhere. Jacques Marquette was first to put
the island on a white man's map....

If the copper came by water to the forest paths,
it came by long canoe along the shores
of Huron into Lake St. Clair and then Detroit

where the trail curved into Canada.
Was Father Claude Allouez, the Jesuit, correct
who said of them who called

themselves *Neshnabek* and the other
tall Algonquins at Green Bay that golden copper
shapes were manitous, that queerly

wrought and efficacious metals were the secret
household gods of Potawatomies
who worshipped, like grave alchemists, the sun?

4. Saint-Lusson, Green Bay

The King of all these Frenchmen *was* the sun,
or so he liked to say, and Saint-
Lusson's vain oratory blazed with a brightness

at Green Bay outshining any local *kiktowenene's*.
But did he know to whom he spoke? Did
he know the phratries and the clans? Who was Bear

and who was Wolf or Bird, Elk or Moose or Fox?
He knew less of them than they knew
of the ones who built the mounds and made the trails

and mined the copper glowing in their lodges.
Chaskyd the ventriloquist? Wabino
eating fire? What was sleight of hand & superstition

to these soldiers of the King who sang *Vexilla Regis*
and the Jesuits who dreamed theocracy
and sought to make of these great lakes a Paraguay?

Nicholas Perrot, himself a spirit-power
said every Shaman there, assembled lines of Winnebagoes,
Potawatomies, Menomonies and Sauks before the *engagés,*

and cynical *coureurs de bois,* before the priests, before
the silken Saint-Lusson. *Vive Le Roi,* he said,
picking up a clod of earth and brandishing his sword....

Did Wiske smile on these transactions, throw
tobacco on the fire? And did his brother Chibyabos chant
beyond the sunset names that sounded there

like Onangizes and Onontio? *Vive Le Roi, and hail
the highest and most mighty monarch and
most Christian King of France and of Navarre*

*for whom I take possession of this place Sault St. Marie
and also lakes Superior and Huron also
Manitoulin also all the countries rivers lakes and*

streams contiguous adjacent thereunto both those dis-
covered and the ones we will discover
in their length & breadth & bounded only by the seas

declaring to the nations living there that they
from this time forth are vassals
of his Majesty bound by laws & customs which are his.

Then Allouez harangued them about Jesus.
Francis Parkman writes: "What remains of sovereignty
thus pompously proclaimed?

Now and then
the accents of some straggling boatman or
a half-breed vagabond—

this and nothing more."

5. Making of the Rivers and the Prairies

Before that rhetoric, that epigraph,
gushing of the ancient, unheard waters all along
the terminal moraine. Before the melt,

Maumee ice flow inching toward a Wabash
where no water ran, a Saginaw
into a dry Dowagiac. Before an unbound Kankakee,

glacial borders pressing ice lobes out
to flood the valley where no valley was, to spread
the drift two hundred feet and more above

Corniferous, Devonion and Trenton rock.
Before the flood, copper manitous locked up in stone
on distant islands not enisled

before the miners who would dig for them
where no mines were and build the pregnant mounds
by forest trails that were not blazed.

Before the forest trails, before the oak & ash,
path of the moraine: sand & boulders,
quartzite, clay and till...

Before the Potawatomies. Before the French.
Before the Studebaker &
the Bendix and the Burger Chef....

                    •

                    10,000 years ago
the Erie ice, the Saginaw,
the Michigan converged just here.

Hills and ranges fixed the contours then.
Basins formed, and runoff made
two rivers wider than the Mississippi.

Tributaries broke through lateral moraines.
The Elkhart and the Yellow rivers
drained away the last of Maumee glacier—

no waters yet could run off to Desplaines.
When they did, the two great rivers
slowed—silted up their valleys with debris

and changed their names.
Turning on itself, Dowagiac became its former
tributary, flowing to Lake Michigan.

Kankakee at flood time
emptied into the immense abandoned channel,
flowed on to St. Joseph, left

an ice gorge, then a sand bar and a bluff
here at Crum's Point.
Drainage opened to the east

all the way beyond the lakes to the St. Lawrence.
Water levels fell, channels
slowly narrowed, and the River of Miamis

took its present course. Curving to the south.
Flowing to the north.
Rising where it fell in the beginning.

So Crum's Point burst its ice-dam and
the Kankakee flowed mostly with the stronger
new and narrow river now.

Silted up to fourteen feet, the site
of a confluence sealed itself with rock
and sand and soil: made

a watershed on the continental divide.
Above, the level sand plain. And below, the marsh:
Seignelay south-west, & Illinois.

From a millennium of glacial drift, the prairies
now had formed: Portage, Palmer
Sumption...

Terre Coupée....

•

But on these waters:
Could you sail a ship?
And on this land: *Found an empire now*

      surrounded on the north and east by oak & hickory? On the south adjoining: scattered clumps of alders, willow bushes native to these soils. The prairie reached from portage landing two and one half miles, three & more from the nearest eastern verge. To the west & south, the vast expanse of grass and marsh appeared as one great plain. Deep into the west, a stretch of rolling timber....

6. The Boat-Maker's Tale

He'd sent the Griffin on back to Niagara
loaded with the furs he thought
would pay his debts....
                Colbert walked in shadows

at Versailles, the river to be named for him
named otherwise by Onangizes, called
himself, like Colbert's king, the shimmering sun.

Frontenac, Onnontio to Green Bay's Ouilamette
and all the rest of Gigos clan,
dreamed a map of colonies and little forts

stretching from above St. Joseph on the lake
down the river of Miamis
to the marshy waters of that languid

tributary to be named one day for Seignelay
whose own necrology of ships
made him Minister among the idle admirals

in the shipyards and the ports of France.
Stretching farther still ...
Stretching well beyond that river to the one

that only Joliet and Père Marquette
among the French had ever seen & named & spoken of
saying that *no land at all no*

country would be better suited to produce
whatever fruits or wheat or corn
than that along this river that the wild cattle

never flee that one finds some 400 in a herd
that elk & deer are almost every-
where and turkeys promenade on every side....

From the day a man first settled here
that man
could start to plow....
                          But Cavelier, La Salle,

had sent the Griffin on back to Niagara.
He'd build a second ship
to sail down the rivers he would find....

For he himself had said in Paris, sounding
just like Père Marquette, *it's all*
so beautiful and fertile, free from forests

full of meadows brooks and rivers all
abounding there in fish & game
where flocks and herds can even be left out

all winter long. All winter long!
And it was nearly winter now in Michillimackinak.
The King had said to him *We have received*

with favor a petition in your name and do
permit your exploration
by these presents signed with our own hand

but now he was in debt. Migeon, Charon—
they'd seized the beaver pelts
and even skins of skunks—Giton, Pelonquin!

Names of enemies. But there was Henri Tonty here;
there was, indeed, Count Frontenac.
These he'd name against the plotting creditors.

The ship will fly above the crows, he'd said,
his patron governor's heraldic mast-
head besting Jesuits in a Niagaran dream of power.

He had his Récollets to do whatever of God's work
there was. Hennepin, who strapped
an altar on his back and cured the fainting

Father Gabriel with a confection of hyacinths!
and Gabriel himself; and Zénobe.
They'd sung *Te Deum* well enough upon the launching.

He'd have them sing a good deal more than that—
Exaudiat, Ludovicus Magnus!—
once they'd reached the Colbert's mouth, the sea.

The ship *had* nearly flown across the lakes.
In spite of an ungodly pilot
and in spite of god knows dreadful storms

she'd been the equal of the Erie and the Huron.
How she'd sailed out beyond Niagara!
Her canvas billowed & she fired her five small guns

to the astonishment of Iroquois along the banks.
Then a freshening northwest wind.
Down the lake and to Detroit's narrow straights

she sailed until she met a current there strong
as the bore before the lower Seine—
and twelve men leapt ashore to pull her over, through.

They marvelled at the prairies to the east & west
and stopped to hunt, and hung their
guyropes full of fowl and drying bearskins.

From wild grapes the priests prepared communion wine.
Then they were in Huron where the gale
attacked them and they brought down mainyards, tacked

with trysail, then lay long to the till.
The pilot blasphemed damnably while all the rest
cried out to Anthony of Padua

who calmed the winds and brought the ship to port
at Michillimackinak beside
the mission of St. Ignace, Père Marquette's fresh grave.

That was in the early autumn when the Ottawa
and Huron fishing fleets
were strung across the lakes from Saint Marie du Sault

to Keweenwa, from Mackinac to Onangizes' islands
in Green Bay. He'd worn his scarlet coat
with its gold lace and flown the banner of the king

while all his men fired muskets & he stepped ashore.
That was autumn, when the sun
still burned their necks & missionaries harvested.

But it was nearly winter now and he would be he said
in Illinois country when the rivers froze.
Heavy clouds blew in from Canada on northern winds.

The ship had sailed away. And so they
set forth on the lake in four canoes: fourteen men
who bore with them a forge & carpenters' &

sawyers' tools to build the Griffin's twin
beside a fort they'd also build on high ground near
the navigable lower Illinois.

They cried out to each other in the dark.
For it was dark before they were across the lake.
It stormed again as when the Griffin

rocked and shook on Huron, waves against the fragile
birchbark, rain in their red eyes.
Anvil and bellows, iron for nails and bolts,

pit-saws, arms, and merchandise for gifts
and trade when they had reached the Illinois town below
the portage weighed them down.

Gunsmith, blacksmith, joiner, mason, master-
builder Moyse Hillère—
they paddled for the further shore with Cavelier

and three priests and the guide. Half of them
were cousins to *coureurs de bois*
and would desert. Two of them were felons.

All of them washed up together with the breaking
waves beside
the mouth of the Miamis

        and gorged on grapes and wild haws &
on the carcass of a deer that had been killed by wolves.

Here they stayed for twenty days, and built a tiny fort,
and spiked the hill they built it on. They took nine
soundings of the river's mouth, marking out the pas-
sage that a ship might take with buoys and bearskin
flags. The first brief snow blew in across the lake well
before December and ice began to form along the riv-
er's edge. Occasionally, La Salle's Mohegan guide
could find a deer to kill, or bear, and brought them
meat; but food was scarce and all of them began to urge
La Salle to press on to the portage and to Illinois or
Miami camps where they might find, in covered pits, a
gleaming hoard of winter's corn. When Tonty finally
came with men who had been sent ahead from Fort
Niagara but had scattered in the woods, the party num-
bered thirty-four. Four were left behind with messages
and maps for those who would arrive to reinforce them
when the Griffin sailed back past Michillimackinak and
down Lake Michigan & anchored here. If the Griffin
wasn't lost. If the furs to pay off creditors had not been
stolen by the pilot and his men. If all of them had not
sailed straight to join the outlaw trader Dan Du Lhut at
Kamalastigouia up in Thunder Bay.

Nous embarquâmes, wrote Hennepin, *le troisième Decem-
bre. Avec trente hommes... Dans huit canots.* They were
John Boisrondet, L'Espérance de la Brie, La Roussel-
ière, La Violette, Picard du Gay, Etienne Renault,

Michel Baribault, Bois d'Ardeene, Martin Chartier, Noel le Blanc, the nailer called La Forge, the Indian guide they called Oui-Oui-La-Meche, and those with names now known to all or names now known to none. They took up paddles once again, prepared to travel on, to shoulder their canoes along the portage trail if they could find it. Had it been spring, had it been high summer, the fields and woods that lined the river's channel would have blossomed for them, fruited like the prairies on the east and west of the Detroit straights when they pulled the Griffin through to Huron and the priests made wine. And when at last they reached the portage, they would have seen tall cedars, oaks, and water-elms; in a ravine declining from high ground they would have seen along the curving trail splashes of the reds and blues of wild forest flowers; flocks of plovers, snipe, might have flown above the trees to land beside the standing cranes in fields of wild rice in fens the far side of the watershed across the prairie with its elk and deer and buffalo which traders would begin to call one day the *Parc aux Vaches*. But it was winter; they saw none of this. They saw the skulls and bones of animals, a bleak gray plain; they lugged their eight canoes and forge and iron and anvil up the hill and then along the portage path behind La Salle who brooded on the Griffin in the melancholy, willful, isolated silence of his mind, La Salle whose men, with five exceptions, would forsake his vision and his surrogate at Fort Crevecoeur—39 degrees and 50 minutes latitude exactly on his fine Parisian astrolabe—and daub in tar-black letters on the planking of the half-built river boat: *Nous Sommes Tous Sauvages*.

The man who followed him in many ways was like him, and read his words, and read the words and followed all the trails of others who had passed this way before he did himself, but after him who was the first to come and was the object of his search. Charlevoix he read, and La Hontan. Tonty's own account, and Hennepin's, and all of La Salle's letters both to Canada and France. Transcripts, depositions. He too knew about insatiable ambition, pride and isolation, subduing all to an inflexibility of purpose. When his chronic and mysterious illness made his head swim and his joints swell, made his eyes so sensitive to light he could not read, his nights so sleepless that he could not even dream his shattered double's thousand mile trek from the lower Illinois back to Montreal, he had his friends read *to* him, tried to comprehend their strange pronunciations of the language of the texts and maps and manuscripts *de la France Septentrionale* which he followed to the Kankakee or Seignelay and then beyond....

Terres tremblantes, sur lesquelles on peut à peine marcher he read, and wrote how "soon they reached a spot where oozy saturated soil quaked beneath their tread. All around were clumps of alder-bushes...pools of glistening water *une espèce de mare* and in the midst a dark and lazy current, which a tall man might bestride...twisting like a snake among the reeds and rushes and...*il a faut continuellement tourner*... They set canoes upon this thread of water and embarked their baggage and themselves and pushed on down the sluggish streamlet looking at a little distance like men who sail on land... Fed by an increasing tribute of the spongy soil it widened to a river *presque aussi large que la Marne*, and they floated on their way into a voiceless, lifeless solitude of boundless marshes overgrown with reeds....

At night they built their fire on ground made firm by frost
quelques mottes de terres glacées

and bivouacked among rushes..."

7. Convergence... & Dispersion

Behind La Salle, before his blinking chronicler,
these others came. They came
to undo all designs of Tisha and his friends,

all designs conceived by Jesuit or Récollet
or empire builder in Quebec
or dreamed beneath Starved Rock among the Illinois.

These others came on urgent journeys of unmaking
and from very far away
but very fast and very quietly and no one knew.

They travelled not so much by river routes & streams
as by the trails. They came
because the French and their Algonquin allies

were establishing an iron monopoly
on furs which handsome ladies like Madame d'Outrelaise
and Madame Frontenac—*les divines*

they called them at Versailles—liked to drape around
their pink & chilly shoulders
when in Paris they would hear, at Arsanal,

the private recitations of Racine and Molière
or walk the Louvre along Perrault's
great colonnade, or walk le Brun's new gallery nearby.

These others walked the narrow trails
from Mohawk lodges on through busy Onondaga country
to the Senecan frontier—

These others were the Iroquois.
And when La Salle objectively took note of 1680's comet
wondered at in Paris and the calculated

object of Sir Isaac Newton's will,
Increase Mather wrote upon the theocratic tablet of his soul:
A Portent! Well, it may have been.

Trade among the openings of oak and on the open prairie
would be anything but free.
And so they leaned into their journey, east to west,

and put a price upon it.
Over trails between the rivers flowing to the lakes
& those that flowed into the Susquehanna south—

then across the Seneca & north beyond Cayuga
to the watershed between Ontario and Erie, to Niagara.
Canadasegy, Canadaragey, Canawagus—

villages on ley lines into which their dancing feet
trod magic from the Hudson river west
and to Detroit....

                    •

                    Behind the Iroquois,
        the English and the Dutch.
Behind the Dutch and English, the Americans.

Braddock, Washington. Clark & Wayne & Harrison.
The Iroquois trails and the Sauk
widened to accommodate the marching of militias—

For convergence of new peoples in procession
down new roads, dispersion's
an express condition, and diaspora's required....

Pontiac's conspiracy. Tecumseh's genius
and the wild hallucinations of the Shawnee prophet
in his Prophetstown. Black Hawk for an hour.

All the rest is trade—wagons made
by Clem and Henry Studebaker in a town Coquillard
founded for the Astors.

Oh, and Cooper's wooden Indians.
Standing near the banks of local rivers in his book
of 1848, they decorate a prairie

modelled now on European parks mown by gardeners
who themselves become like trees
on the green & flowering stage which they prepare

a decade after the removal of the Potawatomis.
They stand there like Pokagon, last
okama of the lakes whose little band did not accept

the Treaty of Chicago engineered by Billy Caldwell
but remained in his protection
and in his most pious Christian prayers, and even

in his fiction ghosted by a local lawyer's wife
whose husband pressed his claims
in every court. Cooper's stagecoach, meanwhile,

clatters past the Walker Tavern on the old Sauk trail
that's become the route of Western's
bright red buckboards & their Concord Coaches from Detroit.

The aging author whose new book will be dismissed
for tedious didacticism & a meager plot
engages Mrs. Martineau from London in a civil conversation

interrupted by her not infrequent jottings in a diary
about how wisely planned
and prettily she finds this road from Niles

which the Iroquois took to slaughter Illinois women
at Starved Rock and which, from
Ypsilanti down to Edwardsburg and then beyond

80,000 western emigrants began to stream by 1838 or 39.
We cross St. Joseph's River,
Mrs. Martineau observes, *upon a ferry towed by ropes.*

And as the clever horses pull us up the bank
we find ourselves in Indiana territory. She glances up
at Cooper who, in turn, acknowledges her smile.

The stagecoach travels on. Arriving from Fort Wayne,
and heading north & west along
what still they call the Dragoon Trail, the U. S. mail...

while ahead of it, turning just in front of Cooper's
coach on Michigan, honking Studebakers
and the children marching smartly off in little groups

before the dignitaries—councilmen & mayor
& some Elks & Shriners dressed to look like Potawatomi
and Illinois elders—

and everybody smiling at the camera
as if this were
some kind of local pageant

　　　•

　　　& they gathered near the portage trail
to commemorate La Salle in a depression.
Hoover, says the Mayor, will employ honest citizens

to build a great historic monument. A corner
stone is laid. Massed bands of high school students play,
choirs singing in the cold...*Semper Fidelis.*

December 5, 1679. *Queleques mottes de terres glacées.*
Eight years later and
La Salle was murdered by conspirators in Texas.

A bell tower rises, in a man's imagination,
some two hundred feet. (The monument was never built.)
On the river, down below the pageant,

in a man's imagination or before him on his page
Now and then
the accents of a straggling boatman

or a half-breed vagabond
this &
nothing more....

A Compostela Diptych

For Guy Davenport and John Peck

Part I: France

I

Via Tolosona, Via Podiensis.
There among the tall and narrow cypresses,
the white sarcophagi of Arles

worn by centuries of wind & sun,
where Charlemagne's lieutenants it was said
lay beside Servilius & Flavius

and coffins drifted down the Rhone
on narrow rafts to be unloaded by St. Victor's monks,
they walked: Via Tolosona.

Via Podiensis: They walked as well from
Burgundy through the Auvergne,
slogged along volcanic downland up into Aubrac

and on through Languedoc to Conques
and gazed into the yellow morning light falling
from above the central axis through

the abbey's lantern tower
and praised St. Foy, and praised as well
with Aimery Picaud their guide

the names of certain travelers
who had long before secured the safety of their way
and also other ways: Via Podiensis,

Via Lemosina, Via Turonensis.
They crossed the Loire at Tours and at Nevers,
walking toward Bordeaux or

from St. Leonard and St. Martial of Limoges
to Périgord and to Chalosse.
At Tours beside the sandy, wide & braided river

they would rest a while and bathe
or seek the narrow shoals nearby & shallow streams
that ran between. Here St. Martin's

shrine had outfaced Abd-al-Rahman
and they prayed at his basilica remembering
the ninety thousand Moors

beaten back to Córdoba before Almansor
took the bells of Santiago
for his candle-sticks, hung them highly

in his elegant great mosque & upside down.
His singers sang of it.
These walking also sang: Via Lemosina,

Via Turonensis: they sang the way along the ways.
They sang the king: *Charles li reis,*
ad estet en Espaigne...Tresqu'en la mer

conquiste la terre altaigne. Trouvères, jongleurs,
langue d'oïl, langue d'oc: of love
& war, the Matamoros & the concubine at Maubergeon.

And there was other song—song sung inwardly
to a percussion of the jangling
manacles and fetters hanging on the branded

heretics who crawled the roads
on hands and knees and slept with lepers under
dark facades of abbeys

& the west portals of cathedrals with their zodiacs.
These also sang: as had
the stern young men, their sheep or cattle

following behind, when up
to high summer pasture they would carry
from the scoria-red waste

a wooden image of their black and chthonic mother
burned in her ascent up out of
smoking Puy-de-Dome (or her descent

from very heaven: Polestar's daughter urging
them to Finisterre....
                                    Whichever way

they came they sang.
Whatever song they sang they came.
Whichever way they came, whatever song they sang,

they sang and walked together on the
common roads: Via Lemosina,
Via Turonensis; Via Tolosona, Via Podiensis.

II

Dorian, Phrygian, Lydian—
modes in diatonic sequence which would order
the response & antiphon at Cluny:

authentic, plagal; plagal and authentic—
hypodorian, hypomixolydian—
Magnificat! Magnificat anima mea Dominum.

And canticles in stone carved in capitals
to honor every mode
in which the honor of this Lady might

be chanted, melismatic even,
graced the choir itself in St. Hugh's hall
where someone wrote the book

sending walkers down the roads to Santiago.
Whose creation Aimery Picaud?
Whose persona Turpin? *The Codex Calixtinus!*

Book that wrought a miracle of power?
or book that answered it and echoed it, reflected
power trans-Pyrenean and uncanny,

causality determined by no human hand?
Did Santiago draw his pilgrims to his shrine,
or did the Monks of Cluny push?

Far from the basilica, far from
the *corona* with its hundred lamps & more lighted
there to brighten Pentecost or Easter, far

from the twelve arcades of double pillars,
the goldsmith's workshop & the bearded lutenist beside
the dancing girl celebrating in their frozen

artistry the artistry of monophonic provenance
which answered every gesture
of the vestured celebrant—and far, far before

the carving of a single capital,
the scribbling of a single line of Latin in a single book,
the hammering of gold, the glazing

of an ornament, the singing of the kyrie or gloria,
the censing of the host,
a strange boat arrived off Finisterre....

(Or so they say. Or so they said
who made the book.) The boat came from Jerusalem
without a sail, without a rudder,

without oars. It bore his head beside his body
who had caught it when the sword
of Herod dropped it in his open hands.

It bore his two disciples. As they neared
the land beneath the *campus stellae*
where the lord of every geste would heave his

spear into the surf, drawn across the Pyrenees
by virtue of this other who would lie down now
for some eight hundred years—son of Zebedee

and Salomé, brother of St. John, son of Thunder
born into Galicia—
a bridegroom riding to his wedding reined

his horse in, stared a moment at the little boat,
galloped straight into the tranquil sea.
When horse and rider rose, both were covered with

the scallop shells that were his sign, his
awaiting Cluny and his cult
(the carving of the capitals, the canticles in stone,

the singing of the antiphons,
the scribbling of the Latin in his lenten book)
but also *hers*—

Magnificat! Magnificat anima mea Dominam—
who rose up on a scallop shell
to dazzle any bridegroom staring at whatever sea.

So it began. So they said it had begun.
A phase (a phrase (a moment in
the spin of some ephemeride (a change

not even in the modes of music
from the Greek
to the Gregorian....

    (And chiefly with an aim to rid the south of
Moors, to rid it of the Mozarabic taint in liturgies and
chants, to blast the peasant heretics following the Gnos-
tic light of Avila's Priscillian. And then? Then the casti-
gations of Bernard, the smashings of the Huguenots,
the marshals of Napoleon on the mountain trails, the
slow dismantling of the abbey for its stone, the twists of
floral patterns on the broken columns standing in the
ruined granary, the Shell Oil station on the highway

through the pass. And at the restaurant by the river in St-Jean-Pied-de-Port (Michelin: 2 stars), good coquilles St. Jacques...

III

Aimery Picaud to those who walked:
Beware the Gascons and beware the Basques:
drink only from this well, never

drink from that: these boatmen on that river
will deceive you: trust
only those who ply the other one: and if

you cross the mountains through
the path of Cize, be warned of Ostabat where men
appear with sticks to block your way

and then by force extract an unjust toll:
these men are fierce, the country they inhabit barbarous,
their tongue terrifies the hearts of all who hear:

God they call *Urcia,* bread is *orgui,* wine is *ardum:*
may the rich who profit from their tolls
and fares, the lords above the rivers & the king of Aragon,

Raymonde de Solis and Vivien d'Aigremont,
atone by long and public penitance; may any priest
who pardons them be smitten with anathema:

Depraved they are, perverse and lecherous,
destitute of any good; the men
and women show their private parts to pilgrims,

fornicate with beasts; the men kiss the vulva
of both wife and mule. When a man
comes in a house he whistles like a kite, & when

he lurks behind the rocks or trees
he hoots out like an owl or howls like a wolf:
Beware these Gascons & beware these Basques.

But at the gate of Cize rejoice!
From this high peak you gaze down at the western ocean,
at the frontiers of Castille & Aragon & France.

Here with axe and mattock, spade
and other tools Charlemagne's companions built a road
into Galicia: May their souls rest

in peace, and may the souls also of those others
who in times of Aldefonso & Calixtus
worked upon the road and made it safe rest in peace:

André, Roger, Avit, Fortus, Arnault,
Etienne and Pierre, who built the bridge again
over the Mino: for them, eternal peace.

If you cross the Somport pass
you come to several towns: to Borce first and
then to Canfranc, Jaca, Osturit,

Tiermas of the royal baths, and Monreal.
You will meet the road from Cize
at Puente-La-Reina. Estella has good bread,

good wine & meat & fish, and all things
there are plentiful. Past Estella flow the waters
of the Ega, sweet and pure, as are

these other rivers I now name: the Cea
by Sahagún, the Esla by Mansilla,
the Torio by León and near the Jewish camp.

If you come by Arles and Les Alischamps
you will see more tombs of marble
than you would believe carved in Latin dialect

spread before you more than one mile long
& one mile wide. If you come
by Arles you must seek the relics of

St. Honoratus and St. Gilles.
Between the branches of the Rhone, at Trinquetaille,
stands the marble column where the people

tied St. Honoratus and beheaded him.
He caught his head and threw it in the Rhone where
angels bore it to the sea and

on to Cartageña where it rests in glory
& performs great miracles.
Who would fail to kiss the altar of St. Gilles?

Who would fail to tell the story of his
pious life? On the golden coffer there behind his
altar in the second register are Aries,

Taurus, Gemini and Cancer with the other signs
winding among golden flowers on a vine.
A crystal trout stands erect there on his tail.

May the Hungarians blush to say they have
his body. May the monks of Chamalières be confounded.
I, Arnauld du Mont, transcribe today

the writings of Picaud, describe the roads the
states the castles towns and mountains
waters wells and fishes men and lands and saints

the habits customs routes and weathers in this
fifth book of the *Codex Calixtinus*
on the stages of the way to Santiago.

IV

From Mont Saint-Michel to Sens,
from Besançon to Finisterre, a darkness fell at noon,
the walls of houses cracked, down

from all the bell towers tumbled bells.
In the encampment, flames leapt from spears of ash & apple,
hauberks buckled, steel casques burst,

bears and leopards walked among the men in Charles' dream.
For so he dreamed. Dreamed within
a dream Roland's requiem before the ships

of Baligant sailed up the Ebro,
their mastheads and their prows decked and lighted
through the night with lamps and rubies

in the story that Turaldos tells.
(From Ostabat, the Port of Cize, Val Carlos—then
the high road trod by Gascons & the Basques:

The road below was made by strangers and their armies.
Turonensis, Lemosina, Podiensis:
Straight to Spain each one through Roncevaux.)

They came to him among the Saxons saying:
join us against the Omayyads
at Saragossa: march with us to Abd-al-Rahman's hall.

It was Suleiman himself, governor of Barcelona,
Abbasid and loyal to
the Caliphate of Baghdad. Charles made it a crusade.

Burgundians and Lombards, Goths and Provençals,
Austrasians and Bavarians
loyal to the Reich found themselves conscripted

for the Frankish Blitzkreig. For this was *Hereban:*
this was draft trumpeted by missi
all across Imperium: this was all incumbent on

vicarius and count. And so they came.
They came with sumpter, destrier,
& palfrey; they came with cooks & carpenters & sheep.

They marched away looking like a tribe of nomads
followed by the peddlers & the jugglers,
the singers & the whores. And crossed the mountains

at the Port of Cize. In the Cluny version
there is no Suleiman & no alliance.
Everything is supernatural power. The walls of Pamplona

fall at Charles' approach. He curses
and Luçerna is a great salt lake in which there swims
a single large black bass.

Turpini Historia Karoli: "I am James the son of
Zebedee whom Herod slew. My body
is Galicia. Seek me in this dream & I will be your stay.

My body is Galicia; my soul a field of stars."
Off he marched to Compostela;
At Finisterre he threw his spear into the sea.

In the lives of Einhard and The Stammerer, the facts;
In the *Geste* and *Codex,*
fear and hope and song:—

From Mont Saint-Michel to Sens,
from Besançon to Finisterre, a darkness fell at noon,
the walls of houses cracked, down

from all the bell towers tumbled bells.
In the encampment, flames leapt from spears of ash & apple,
hauberks buckled, steel casques burst,

bears and leopards walked among the men in Charles' dream.
For so he dreamed. Dreamed within
a dream Roland's requiem before the ships

of Baligant sailed up the Ebro,
their mastheads and their prows decked and lighted
through the night with lamps and rubies

in the story that Turaldos tells.
(From Ostabat, the Port of Cize, Val Carlos—then
the high road trod by Gascons & the Basques:

The road below was made by strangers and their armies.
Turonensis, Lemosina, Podiensis:
Straight to Spain each one through Roncevaux....

Before the Codex made at Cluny, the Capitularies;
before the pseudo-Turpin, Turpin.
And afterwards the song. Afterwards the echoing of
    Roland's horn.

The nine hundred meters to the Vierge d'Orisson.
The planted crosses like a harbor full of masts.
Afterwards the E.T.A.,

the slogans of the separatists,
Afterwards the sabotaged refinery, the blown-up train.
Afterwards the dawn escape across the pass.

From Mont Saint-Michel to Sens,
from Besançon to Finisterre, a darkness fell at noon,
the walls of houses cracked, down

from all the bell towers tumbled bells.

V

Aoi.
Pax vobiscum, pax domini,
Aoi.
      Ainsi soit il.

And Charles murdered fourteen hundred Saxons
after Roncevaux, cutting off their heads,
when no one would reveal the hiding place of

Widukind, when no one would convert. A northern
paradigm for slaughters in the south?
At the far end of the trail, before there was a trail,

there were tales told: narratives of gnosis
whispered themselves north
to bleed in Roussillon when shepherds saw the

flocks of transmigrating souls walk among their
sheep looking for good company
and habitation....
      Even thus Galicia's Priscillian:

Executed 385 by Evodius, Prefect appointed
by the tyrant Maximus,
at the urging of Ithacius, his fellow Bishop....

The soul, then, of its own will doth come to earth,
passing through the seven heavens, and
is sown in the body of this flesh. Or would one rather

say, as did Orosius to St. Augustine: "Worse than
the Manichees!" And the Saint: "Light!
which lies before the gaze of mortal eyes, not only

in those vessels where it shines in its purest state,
but also in admixture to be purified:
smoke & darkness, fire & water & wind...its own abode."

Along the Via Tolosona to Toulouse and then beyond
they told the tales: tunics of human flesh,
penitential wandering, sparks hereticated, vestures of decay.

They praised the seal of the mouth,
the seal of the belly and the hand; the demiurge
was author of this world;

among the rocks and trees, among the sheep
& cattle, they acknowledged each
the aeon that was only an apparent body, only born

apparently into the pitch and sulphur of a human shape
to utter human words. The words
they uttered and the tales they told were strange:

>   *...when I was once*
> *a horse, I lost my shoe between*
> *the stones & carried on unshod the whole night long.*
>
> *Cloven to the navel by this wound got of a Moor,*
> *I speak to him alone who goes out*
> *with the dead, the messenger of souls*
>
> *who saw the lizard run into the ass's skull....*
> *The Ram presides above the head,*
> *the Twins behind the loins....*
>   Were these voices then

an echo of a field of force counter to
the leys on which the houses of St. James aligned
themselves from north of Arles into Spain?

71

No Cluniac reform or Romanesque adornment to
the dogma from the rustic prentices of old Priscillian
dead eight hundred years before their time;

no chant in diatonic mode, in good Gregorian, but
diabolic danger here. This
called out for Inquisition and for blood.

Across all Occitania, across the Languedoc
and down the Via Tolosona spread
the news: Béziers was ruined and destroyed,

fifteen thousand fell before the walls & in the town
where mercenaries heard the knights cry out
to conjure holocaust: *kill them all; God will know his own.*

At Bram, Monfort gouged the eyes out, cut
the nose and upper lip off all survivors of his siege,
leaving just one man with just one eye

to lead his friends to Cabaret.
This was orthodox revenge. This was on the orders
of a man called Innocent.

Raymond of Toulouse, driven from his city,
fled to England, then returned
through Spain where troops passed down the Somport Pass

along the Tolosona to link up with his confederates,
the counts of Foix and of Comminges.
The chronicles explain that *everyone began*

to weep and rushed toward Raymond as he entered
through the vaulted gates to kiss
his clothes, his feet, his legs, his hands.

He appeared to them like one arisen from the dead .
At once the population of the town
began to mend the walls that Monfort had torn down.

Knights and burgers, boys and girls, great and small,
hewed and carried stones while troubadours
sang out their mockery of France, of Simon, of his son.

It was not enough. Though Simon died
outside the walls, the French king and Pope Honorious
concluded what the Monforts

and Pope Innocent began. Behind the conquerors
there came Inquisitors; with
the Inquisitors, denunciations, torture and betrayal.

But in the mountains and along the shepherds' paths
leading to and from the Tolosona trail,
the old tales nonetheless were whispered still

far from cities and the seneschals, far from
Bernard Gui, his book & his Dominicans.
The cycle of transhumance led itinerant *perfecti*

there among gavãches as far from their own ostals
as the Ariège is from Morella,
the wide Garonne from Ebro's northern bank & winter camp.

...tunics of human flesh,
penitential wandering, sparks hereticated, vestures
of decay....

Among the rocks and trees, among the sheep
and cattle, they acknowledged each
the aeon that was only an apparent body, only born

apparently into the pitch & sulphur of a human shape
to utter human words.
And in Galicia, beneath the nave, restless with the centuries,

the east-facing tombs out of all alignment with
the Roman mausoleum & supporting walls
take up proximity below the bones in Santiago's vault

to something holy. The martyred heretic of Trier?
Aoi.
Pax vobiscum, pax domini.

    Aoi. Ainsi soit il.

VI

But was it this that found the floriations
in the columns, found in capitals
the dance that found the music of the cloister & the choir,

the song that found the south for Eleanor of Aquitaine?
Trobar, they said: to find.
To find one's way, one's path, to find the song,

to find the music for the song,
to find through stands of walnut, poplar, chestnut,
through meadows full of buttercups

and orchids, over or beside the banks of many rivers
from above Uzerche to well below
the Lot—Vézère, Corrèze, Couze, Dordogne, Vers—

along the paths of sandstone, rust red & pink,
the way through Limousin, through Perigord, all along
the Via Lemosina to a small road leading to

a castle gate, to find a woman in that place
who finds herself in song,
to find a friend, a fellow singer there or on the road.

Or to the north and west, at Poitiers,
along the Touronensis after
Orléans and Tours, to find before the heaths

of Gascony the pine forests and the *plat pays*
of Poitevins who speak the language
sung by William, Lord of Aquitaine, or the Lemosin

of singers who found comfort who found welcome
at his son's court, his who died
at Santiago, and the court of Eleanor his heir

whose lineage from Charlemagne found Angevin Bordeaux.
They came from Albi and Toulouse,
the town of Cahors and the county of Quercy,

but did they find for her and sing
the *Deus non fecit* of the heretic *perfecti* of Provence
or the light from Eleusis

bathing trail and keep and column in its warmth?
Beneath the limestone cliffs of the Dordogne,
past the verges bright with honeysuckle, thyme and juniper,

quarried stone and timber floated toward the sea
on barges by the dark ores of the *causse,*
while salt, fish, and news of Angevin ambition & desire

came on inland from Bordeaux and from Libourne.
From Hautefort, Ribérek; from
nearby Ventadorn, singers found their way to Poitiers.

The sun rains, they sang: *lo soleils plovil,*
while pilgrims in Rocamadour
climbed toward what they sought, singing without benefit

of trobar ric or trobar clus: *midonz, midonz*
in a dazed vision of the lady there,
hunched & black upon a stick fallen from the sky.

To sing, to pray: to find behind them,
south of Ventedorn, of Hautefort, of Cahors & Toulouse,
alignments in the temple of the sun

at Montségur measuring the solstice, measuring
the equinox, dawn light raining
through the eastern portholes of a ship

riding its great wave, counting down the year,
counting down the years, sign by sign
from Aries to The Fish, not to brighten only that

new morning in Provence but latterly to bend
also onto any path
of any who would follow, singing

at the gates of abbeys or below the castle walls
in any language found
where every song was fond

and yet forbidding, forensic as the night.
Did those who sang, do those who sing,
care at all that at the ending of their song,

as at the start, William of Aquitaine,
son of the troubadour, father of the child
they would hail in Poitiers

kneels crying *midonz* to the stars
but finds in Santiago's tomb not the bones of James
but those of the heretic Priscillian?

I am Arnaut who gathers the wind.
I am Arnaut who hunts the hare with the ox.
I am Arnaut who swims against the tide.

                    •

Near Excidieul, long long after Aquitaine
was France, after the end
of what was Angevin, and after the end of the end,

two lone walkers slogged along the road
and spoke of vortices
and things to be reborn

after Europe's latest conflagration. Was it
spring? Was it 1920? The older of the two, trying to
remember after fifty years, could not be sure. It was he
who had crept over rafters, peering down at the
Dronne, once before. He knew that Aubeterre was to
the east, that one could find three keeps outside Mare-
uil, a pleached arbour at Chalais. He knew the roads in
this place. He had walked into Perigord, had seen Nar-
bonne, Cahors, Chalus, and now was once again walk-
ing with his friend near Excidieul. In certain ways he
much resembled the old finders of song, and sang their
songs in his own way and tried to make them new. He
called the other one, his friend, Arnaut, though that
was not his name, and stopped with him beside a castle
wall. He saw above them both, and wrote down in his
book, *the wave pattern cut in the stone, spire-top alevel the
well curb,* and then heard this other say, the sun shining,
the birds singing, *I am afraid of the life after death.* Of a
sudden. Out of the calm and clarity of morning.

He stored the loved places in his memory—the roads,
the keeps beside the rivers, the arbour at Chalais—and
walked in Eleusinian light and through the years to
Rimini and Rome, in darkness on to Pisa in another
war. And after fifty years, and from the silence of his
great old age, he said: *Rucksacked, we walked from Exci-
dieul. When he told me what he feared, he paused, and then he
added: "Now, at last, I have shocked him...."*

Who was Arnaut to gather the wind?

Intercalation

And who, asked the Doctor Mellifluus, were the Cluniacs to gather all *these* things: *deformis formositas ac formosa deformitas*. A wave pattern cut in the stone would have been enough—would have been, perhaps, too much. But apes and monstrous centaurs? half-men and fighting knights? hunters blowing horns? many bodies under just one head or many heads sprouting from a single body? Who were the Cluniacs to gather round them windy artisans to carve their curiosities, to carve chimeras, onto cloister capitals from St. Hugh's Hall to Santiago so that it became a joy to read the marbles and a plague to read the books. The concupiscence of eyes! For he had deemed as dung whatever shone with beauty. (Dung, too, was music and the talk, *humanus et jocundus*, of the monks, or the song of deeds in poetry. The concupiscence of ears! For he'd have silence, silence, save when he would speak, the great voice shaking his emaciated frame near to dissolution and yet echoing through all of Christendom: *Jihad! Jihad!* He looked upon the mind of Abelard, the body of Queen Eleanor, and did not like them. Man of the north, he gazed upon the south and built the rack on which they'd stretch the men of Langedoc after he'd made widows of the women standing horror-stricken outside Vézelay the day a thousand knights called out for crosses.) Contra Dionysius, the pseudo-Areopagite. Contra Saint-Denis. Contra Grosseteste, contra Bonaventure, and before their time. There was, he thundered, darkness in the light. And light in darkness of the fastness, of the desert, of the cave.

And yet, Abbot Suger sighed, thinking on his Solomon and walking in the hall the saint had called the Workshop of Vulcan, the Synagogue of Satan: *dilectio decoris domus Dei....Cross of St. Eloy! Thy chrysolite, thy onyx and thy beryl.* It seemed to him he dwelt in some far region of the mind not entirely on this earth nor yet entirely in the purity of Heaven.... When he looked upon such stones.... When the sun's rays came flooding through the windows of the choir. For he was servant to the Pater Luminum and to the First Radiance, his son. Their emanations drenched so utterly this mortal world that, beholding them polluted even in the vestures of decay, we should rise—*animae*—by the manual guidance of material lights. The onyx that he contemplated was a light, the chrysolite a light, lights the screen of Charlemagne, the Coupe de Ptolemées, the crystal vase, the chalice of sardonyx, and the burnished ewer. Also every carving in the stones—the capitals, the portal of the west facade—and every stone itself, placed with cunning and with reverence according to the rules of proportion on the other stones, and then proportion too, laws invisible made visible by building—place and order, number, species, kind— these were lanterns shining round him which, he said, *me illuminant.*

But to Citeaux, but to Clairvaux: letters which began *Vestra Sublimitas* (and without irony). Acknowledging intemperance in dress, intemperance in food and drink; acknowledging the horses fit for kings and their expensive, sumptuous liveries; superfluities of every kind, excesses which endangered everything, opening the Royal Abbey to the winds of calumny.... He'd move into the smallest cell. He'd walk while others rode. He'd fast.... And yet expand the narthex and reconstruct the choir. Enlarge and amplify the nave. Find a quarry near Pontoise in which they'd cut no longer millstones for their livelihood but graceful columns by the grace of God. He'd execute mosaics on the tympanum, elaborate the crenellations. Hire castors for the objects to be bronzed, sculptors from the Cluniacs to carve in columns tall figures on the splayed jambs. Abolish compound piers and redesign triforia. Raise the towers up above the rose making of the rose itself a fulcrum. Repair the lion's tail that supported until recently the collonette. Repair zodiacal reliefs and, in the crypt, the capitals' eight abacus athemia. In the Valley of Chevreuse, he'd hunt himself for twelve tall trees, trunks sufficient in their height for roof-beams of his new west roof and fell them in the woods with his own axe, and offer thanks. Nor would he renounce the light—whatever letters went to Bernard of Clairvaux—the light proportionate unto itself, order mathematical of all diffusion, infinite in volume and activity, lux and lumen both.

And then at Vézelay, Bernard. Sunny Burgundy. The Via Podiensis and the city on the hill. Bishops, statesmen, peasants hungry for some kind of fair, thugs and mercenaries, Louis King of France who ached for glory and beside him Eleanor. Multitudes so many that they flooded all the fields waiting for the prophet from Clairvaux who would command them (Suger quiet under some far tree; Suger strong for peace). At Sens, he had destroyed Abélard. Now he'd widow all the women of the north. Rhetorician of the Holy War, demagogue of the crusade, he stood outside the abbey where the Pentecostal Christ of Gislebertus, *sol invictus* of the entry to the choir, measures time. But then what time was *this*, what year? Sea-green incorruptible beneath his Abbot's shroud, he numbered hours and souls in strict and occult symmetry. Were days measured once again by Kalends, Nones and Ides? Was solstice equinox and equinox the solstice? Did lunar phases intersect the solar year? Who had carved a column with the *lam* and *alif* of the Holy Name and was it *zenith* now or *nadir* in the Latin's Arabic? Many bodies sprouted from his head and many heads from every weaving body. Hautbois and bass bombarde began to play, shawm and chime and rebec as the voices sang *Fauvel* and *Reis Glorios*. From Mont Saint-Michel to Sens, from Besançon to Finisterre, a darkness fell at noon, the walls of houses cracked, down from all the bell towers tumbled bells. In a far encampment, flames leapt from spears of ash and apple, hauberks buckled, steel casques burst, bears and leopards walked among the men in Bernard's dream. For so he dreamed, even as he spoke. Dreamed within a dream Jerusalem's high requiem before the ships of Saladin sailed south from Tyre, their mastheads and their prows decked and lighted through the night with lamps and rubies in the story that the emirs tell. But everything would not be done at once. He saw emblazoned on a calendar suspended in the sky that it would be the year of Grace— but it would be no year of Grace when he awakened from his grave and found the month Brumaire: Those before him in the field walked straight over his indignant ghost and, shouting out obscenities, burned and looted in the abbey, then marched back down Via Podiensis and the Rue St. Jacques into the capital. All of Paris quaked beneath the church of St. Denis and night revealed itself in which the very stars went out as mobs broke in to take the challices, the vials, the little golden vessels used to serve the wine of the ineffable First Light, and swilled their brandy from those cups, then with clubs and hammers beat them flat. Long lines of priests in vestments led through burning streets a train of mules and of horses laden with patinas, chandeliers and censers from a dozen churches on the Santiago trail, pushed before them carts and wheel-barrows loaded with ciboriums and candle-sticks and silver suns. *Merde!* they shouted. *Vanities!* And tore from

84

roofs and crannies sculpted figures wearing crowns to smash their eyes out and their jaws into a stony chorus of eternal silent screams. Relics torn from reliquaries fed the bonfires and the holy dead themselves were dis-interred. Bells from Languedoc, from Conques, bells that rang above him there at Vézelay, were melted down for cannon and the cannon dragged along the trails into Spain to blast the columns and the capitals, the arms and legs and heads of kingdom come, into the brain of Goya—Vézelay's splayed Christ upon the door become the victims of the Tres de Mayo, the *deformis formositas ac formosa deformitas* of the twisted and uncanny *Disparates,* the black figures on El Sordo's Quinta walls.

...how many years?
The Abbot Suger did not know, but he was Regent.
He set about his work.

Pilgrims set off walking down the Via Podiensis from the church of Julien le Pauvre.

Part II: Spain

I

And from the ninety-second year of the Hegira
and from Damascus
and from the lips of Caliph Walid Abulabas:

permission for Tariq ibn-Ziyad to set forth
from Ceuta in his borrowed ships
to see if what was spoken by Tarif ibn-Malik

and his captives of al-Andalus
was true: serene skies, an excellence of weather,
abundant springs and many rivers,

fruit & flowers & perfume as fine as in Cathay,
mines full of precious metals, tall
standing idols of Ionians amidst extraordinary ruins,

and an infidel weak king despised by tribes & peoples
who but waited to be rendered tributary
to the Caliphate and subject to Koranic law.

And then: collapse of the Visigothic armies
at the battle near Sierra de Retín,
knights' bodies tossed into the rising Barbate

and the footmen with their slings & clubs & scythes
falling before Berber scimitars
days before the Qaysite and Yemeni horsemen

under Musa ibn-Nusayr could even cross
from Jabal Musa. Then the hurried crossing of the straight,
the meeting between Musa and Tariq at Talavera,

89

the occupation of León, Astorga, Saragossa,
and the messenger prostrate before the Caliph in Damascus
saying *Yes! Serene skies, an excellence of weather,*

abundant springs and many rivers, fruit and flowers
and perfume as fine as in Cathay,
mines full of precious metals and, inside this bag

I open for you now, O Caliph,
the severed head of Roderick, king of the Visigoths.
Behold the token of our victory!

Died al-Walid Abulabas in the ninety-sixth year
of the Hegira when, for his troubles,
Musa was condemned by Sulayman to prison & the bastinado

and Tariq ibn-Ziyad disappeared from every chronicle.
But the chronicles themselves go on:
A bad time for Umayyads at home, but every

kind of glory for the jihad in al-Andalus.
Which is why the hungry Umayyad, hunted in the streets
and alleys by the Abbasids, was going there:

the young man hiding in the rushes of Euphrates,
then a silhouetted horseman riding through the desert
    in the night,
the moon on his shoulder, the pole star in his eye.

Landing north of Málaga, he wrote his laws.
Having *crossed the desert*
& the seas & mastered both the wasteland & the waves,

he came into his kingdom, for he was Abd-al-Rahman
and would rule: *no one*
to be tortured, no one to be crucified or burned,

separated from his children or his wife, or anyone
to be despoiled of his holy objects
if in tribute come the golden dinars & the golden wheat

the flour & the barley heaped in bushels on the wagons
to be weighed, the measures
requisite of vinegar and honey, common musk & oil.

And Abd-al-Rahman rebuilt the mosque in Córdoba.
And the second Abd-al-Rahman
Gathered the philosophers and poets, gathered the musicians

and the concubines and wives. And the Sufi at the gates
called his heart a pasture for gazelles, said
he'd come to Córdoba following the camels of his love.

From the columns left by Rome there sprouted upwards
palm-like in oasis the supports
for Allah's double tier of arches, hemisphere

upon the square, fluted dome upon the vault....
When they built the Alcázar &
Madinat al-Zahra, six thousand dressed stones

were called for every day, 11,000 loads of lime & sand.
There were 10,000 workmen, 12,000 mules.
By their kilns and pits, the potters & the tanners,

the armorers and smiths.... Plane, then, on plane...
the surface of each building there
a depth of arabesque, brick and faience overlaid

with geometric pattern & the forms of Kufic & Basmala
lettering interlaced with flowers,
framed by grape vine and acanthus all dissolving

91

strength & weight & structure in a dazzle of idea:
horror vacui: shifting ordering of order
all unseen, water of icosahedron, air of octahedron

fire of tetrahedron on the simple cube of earth,
living carpet in the grid of pathways behind walls,
sunken flower-beds, myrtle bushes

shading tributaries of the central pool and reflection
of the zones and axes of this world
crossing at the intersection where a Ziryab might play

his lute or al-Ghazal recite.... And Abd-al-Rahman
built on Abd-al-Rahman's work, &
Abd-al-Rahman brought it to completion....

Who could have forseen in these expansive years
the squabbling of *taifas*
and Moorish rulers paying tribute to

Alfonso, Sancho, & Rodrigo Díaz El Campeador?
No one walked along the roads
to cross the Aragón where every route converged upon

a single bridge or sang the tales of El Cid & Charlemagne
slogging through Navarre into Castile.
But it was spring. Spring in Burgundy and spring

in all al-Andalus. In Cluny & in Córdoba they carved
stones and sewed the mint & the marjoram;
silkworms hatched & beans began to shoot and all

the apple & the cherry trees flowered white at once.
Water in the aqueducts was fresh as snow
in mountain streams, & everything it irrigated green.

But when the Sufi heard the flute notes in the air
and his disciple asked him
Master, what is that we hear outside the wall?

he looked up from the pile of sand on which he sat
reading the Koran and said:
It is the voice of someone crying for this world

because he wishes it to live beyond its end.
He cries for things that pass.
Only God remains. The music of the flute

Is the song of Satan crying in the desert
for the wells that all run dry,
for the temples & the castles & the caliphates that fall.

II

Via Tolosona, Via Podiensis.
There among the tall and narrow cypresses,
the white sarcophagi of Arles

worn by centuries of wind & sun,
where Charlemagne's lieutenants it was said
lay beside Servilius & Flavius

and coffins drifted down the Rhone
on narrow rafts to be unloaded by St. Victor's monks,
they walked: Via Tolosona.

Via Podiensis: They walked as well from
Burgundy through the Auvergne,
slogged along volcanic downland up into Aubrac

and on through Languedoc to Conques
and gazed into the yellow morning light falling
from above the central axis through

the abbey's lantern tower
and praised St. Foy, and praised as well
with Aimery Picaud their guide

the names of certain travelers
who had long before secured the safety of their way
and also other ways: Via Podiensis,

Via Lemosina, Via Turonensis.
They crossed the Loire at Tours and at Nevers,
walking toward Bordeaux or

from St. Leonard and St. Martial of Limoges
to Périgord and to Chalosse.
At Tours beside the sandy, wide & braided river

they would rest a while and bathe
or seek the narrow shoals nearby & shallow streams
that ran between. And read: *at the gate of Cize*

Rejoice! (Picaud, again Picaud) *And from this peak*
gaze at all the western ocean,
at the frontiers of Castille & Aragón & France.

Here with axe and mattock, spade
and other tools Charlemagne's companions built a road
into Galicia: May their souls rest

in peace, and may the souls also of those others
who in times of Aldefonso & Calixtus
worked upon the road and made it safe rest in peace...

For there were times when all was war.
There was a time, far into the south, when Muhammad's very arm
came to lie and work its magic

in the mosque at Córdoba, a time when Ibn Abi Amir
took it from its jewelled box
and shook it like a spear at Santiago,

made a Via Dolorosa out of every trail in Galicia
and lit a conflagration
which would burn beyond our cities & beyond his time...

From Mont Saint-Michel to Sens,
from Besançon to Finisterre, a darkness fell at noon,
walls of houses cracked, down

from all the bell towers tumbled bells.
In the encampment, flames leapt from spears of ash & apple
hauberks buckled, steel casques burst,

bears and leopards walked among the men in Picaud's dream.
For so he dreamed. Dreamed within
a dream Roland's requiem before the ships

of Baligant sailed up the Ebro,
their mastheads and their prows decked and lighted
through the night with lamps and rubies

in the story that Turaldos tells.
(From Ostabat, the Port of Cize, Val Carlos—then
the high road trod by Gascons & the Basques:

The road below was made by strangers and their armies.
Turonensis, Lemosina, Podiensis:
Straight to Spain each one through Roncevaux.)

And Almanzor al-Allah razed León
and burned the monasteries at Eslonza, Sahagún;
In Navarre, the king gave up his daughter;

counts became his vassals, one by one. On the road
to Córdoba weeping prisoners trod,
year on year from west of Saragossa. In Compostela,

he left not a stone. In Burgos not more than a promise:
That Almoravids would arise to follow him,
fakirs from the deserts of Sahara: that Yusuf ibn-Tashufin

would land in Algeciras, holy & appalling & austere.
His face entirely covered with a veil,
eating only bread and camel's flesh and honey,

he'd annihilate the armies of Alfonso at Sagrajas.
Widows and their children
would go begging on the ashen empty trails

and from Algeciras to the March,
from Marchlands to Finisterre, the dark would fall at noon,
the walls of houses crack, down

from all the bell towers tumble bells.

III

I commend my soul to God, and my remains,
If I be slain by Moors,
to Oña, to whose altar I bequeath

1,600 maravedis, three of my best horses,
two mules, my clothing with the
robes of ciclatoun & my three purple cloaks,

and also two silver goblets. If my vassals
do not bring my body back,
hold them in dishonor, treat them even

as the vassals who had murdered their own lord.
He was ransomed, Count Gonzalo Salvadorez,
and returning—but indeed to Oña to be buried there...

And Ramiro of Navarre was returning—
in an oaken coffin to the church of Saint Maria...
And the men of Logroño to Logroño,

the men of Pamplona to Pamplona...
and the open crypts at Jaca and Sangüesa and at Yesa,
the sepulchers of monasteries on the Ebro,

graves in the churchyards on the Oca and the Aragón,
all began to fill because again
Alfonso had not summoned Don Rodrigo from his exile.

Tañen las campanas en San Pero a clamor
por Castiella.... He has left Castile, the poet sang,
And they rang & pealed the bells,

but he had gone: at Bivar the gate was broken
on its hinges, the porch of his house was empty still;
there were no falcons there, & no molted hawks.

The portals of the city had been shut against him.
When he rode up to Burgos flying sixty pennons, he
   kicked against
the lock, shouted with the strength of sixty heroes

to the people of the city to admit him. But everybody
hid behind his curtained windows.
Alfonso had condemned Rodrigo Díaz, & because of this

Count Gonzalo Salvadorez and Ramiro of Navarre
had died in battle and the king's
beaten army was retreating from the castle at Rueda.

There was worse to come. At Sagrajas, in the south,
as had been foretold.
At Sagrajas, where they beat upon the drums all day.

At Sagrajas, by a tributary of the Guadiana
where Almoravids & the armies of al-Andalus allied themselves
but where Alfonso of Castile & León

failed again to summon Don Rodrigo Díaz from his exile.
Because of that, the Moor could write:
Do thou remember the times of Muhamad Almanzor,

and bring to thy memory those treaties where
thy fathers offered him the homage even of their daughters,
and sent those virgins for their tribute,

even to the far lands of our rule, even into Africa;
Bring this to thy memory before
presuming now to cast thunders against us,

before presuming now to menace us, for we have seen
you marching from the castle at Rueda with
the bodies of Gonzalo Salvadorez & Ramiro of Navarre.

But Alfonso would return the bells of Santiago
to Galicia, and he would boast: *I will*
redeem my word, I will preserve my plighted faith—

and fall upon thy lands with fire and sword
& drive you back into the sea.
There will be no further messages between us...

only the clangour of our arms, the neighing
of the war-horse, the blaring
trumpets and the thundering of atambours.

But riding south without Rodrigo Díaz, he would
soon be riding north—with bodies
of his knights and his confederates, knights & kings

to bury in their lands along the Ebro and the Oca and
the Aragón, where he was riding from Rueda
with the bodies of Gonzalo Salvadorez & Ramiro of Navarre.

Tañen las campanas en San Pero a clamor
por Castiella.... He has left Castile, the poet sang,
and they rang & pealed the bells,

but he had gone: at Bivar the gate was broken
on its hinges, the porch of his house was empty still;
there were no falcons there, & no molted hawks.

The portals of the city had been shut against him.
When he rode up to Burgos flying sixty pennons, he
    kicked against
the lock, shouted with the strength of sixty heroes

to the people of the city to admit him. But everybody
hid behind his curtained windows.
Alfonso had condemned Rodrigo Díaz, & because of this

Count Gonzalo Salvadorez and Ramiro of Navarre
had died in battle and the king's
beaten army was retreating from the castle at Rueda...

and because of this, the king would be routed
at Sagrajas by the Guadiana,
return with the bodies of his knights & his confederates

to bury near Gonzalo Salvadorez & Ramiro of Navarre.

IV

Oit varones una razón! he shouted
in the dusty square,
echoing the *Hoc Carmen Audite* of certain Joculatores,

Joculatores Domini, who stepped around him
and his eager rabble of an audience
to walk beneath the scaffold of the master of Sangüesa

who would freeze him there forever in the stone
even as he left the town
to sing the wayfarers upon their way

from Yesa on through Burgos to León.
On the portal he disports himself with viol & bow,
and also with the lady in a sexy gown

whose other friend is farting in a well beside a cooper
struggling with his heavy barrel.
But on the trail he was quintessential news, was history itself,

and sang the life of Don Rodrigo while El Cid
yet earned the fame to warrant song.
And aged within his story. And grew so very old

his song became a banner among banners
of reconquest: *Oit varones
una razón*—of reconciliation on the Tagus, it might be,

once the hero halted at El Poyo,
once the heralds brought him followers from Aragón & Monreal,
once Minaya sought Alfonso for him

west in Sahagún, west in Carrión,
toward which they walked who'd gathered in the square
beneath the portal of María la Real.

And when Rodrigo rode to meet his king the villagers
& peasants saw, the singer sang
tanta buena arma, tanto buen cavallo corredor—

splendid weapons, swift horses, capes and cloaks
and furs and everyone
vestidos son de colores, all dressed in colors,

underneath the banners
when he stopped on the Tagus, when he fell upon
his face before Alfonso, when he

took between his teeth the grasses of the field—
las yerbas del campo—and wept
great tears as if he had received a mortal wound

and would be reconciled with the earth itself....
as act of faith? Auto de fé?
& near the Tagus once again, Toledo's banners flying

long long beyond him who had come to meet Alfonso
from Valencia & him whose song
became a banner among banners of reconquest?

This *razón* was also sung along the trails, for it was news,
and it was news of conflagration
great as that which burned the northern cities

in the Caliphate: this *razón* was Torquemada's song.
Hoc Carmen Audite.
In conspecto tormentorum.. (As when Don Rodrigo's daughters

103

lash and spurs were shown by their own bridegrooms.
When they entered the grove of Corpes
following the two Infantes back to Carrión near Sahagún.

...bien lo creades
aquí seredes escarnidas en estos fieros montes.
Oy nos partiremos...

And they knew it for a certainty that they
would be tormented,
scourged and shamed and left in that dark place.)

Those abjuring marched with tapers through each town
& wore the sambenito & the yellow robe
embroidered with a black Saint Andrew's cross.

The crier walked before them, crying out
to those who came to watch
the nature of offenses to be punished while

behind them came the paste-board effigies
of those Marranos and Moriscos
who had died of torture, and exhumed bodies

of the heretics dead & buried before Torquemada
reigned at every quemadero:
Hoc Carmen Audite. In conspecto tormentorum....

These we order vicars, rectors, chaplains, sacristans
to treat as excommunicated & accursed for
having now incurred the wrath & indignation of Almighty God

& on these rebels & these disobedient
be all the plagues and maledictions which befell upon
king Pharaoh and his host & may

104

the excommunication pass to all their progeny.
May they be accursed in eating
& in drinking, in waking and in sleeping,

in coming and in going. Accursed be they
in living & in dying & the devil
be at their right hand; may their days be few

and evil, may their substance pass to others,
may their children all be orphans & widows all their wives.
May usurers take all their goods;

May all their prayers be turned to maledictions;
accursed be their bread and wine,
their meat and fish, their fruit & any food they eat;

the houses they inhabit & the raiment that they wear.
Accursed be they unto Satan
and his lords, & these accompany them both night & day....

But far from Toledo, on the road to Sahagún & Carrión,
they told the tales: tunics of human flesh,
penitential wandering, sparks hereticated, vestures of decay.

They praised the seal of the mouth,
the seal of the belly and the hand; the demiurge
was author of this world;

among the rocks and trees, among the sheep
& cattle, they acknowledged each
the aeon that was only an apparent body, only born

apparently into the pitch and sulphur of a human shape
to utter human words. And the Jews
hid their secret practices, and the Arabs likewise theirs,

105

and at the ending of the song, as at the very start,
Don Rodrigo asked his king,
earning thus his exile: *Did you kill your brother?*

Did you collude & commit incest with your sister?
For if you did, all your schemes will fail,
even though I lie prostrate before you eating grass....

Take this oath upon the iron bolt, upon the crossbow.
Otherwise, may peasants murder you—
Villanos te maten, rey; villanos, que no hidalgos;

even though I lie prostrate before you eating grass....

   •

When the singer reached the bridge at Puente la Reina
with the pilgrims who had followed him
for some six hundred years, they met an army:

Soult and Ney & other marshals of Napoleon crossing
into Spain through Roncevaux
and trailing all the engines of their empire....

....bien lo creades
aquí seredes escarnidas en estos fieros montes.
Oy nos partiremos....

Aoi.
Oit varones una razón.
Aoi.

   Hoc Carmen Audite.

V

Soult was at Saldaña on the Carrión
when General Stewart's aide-de-camp walked into Rueda
past the cow-dung fires of peasants

to discover there some eighty horsemen who belonged,
he ascertained, to a division of
Franceski's cavalry. These the light dragoons surrounded

after midnight. General Moore advanced from Salamanca
through Alaejos to Valladolid, & a stolen
sabretache with full intelligence in Marshal Berthier's dispatch

revealed that Junot's infantry had yet to cross the Ebro
and that Ney was still engaged at Saragossa.
On forced march, the British trod December's icy roads

from Toro to Mayorga south of Sahagún.
What pilgrims they became!
Everyone a step-child to some devotee of Sol Invictus,

god of legionaries in whatever expeditionary war,
they billeted beneath the frieze
of Saint María del Camino with its bulls' heads

on abutments of the inner arch, racing horsemen,
and a naked rider on a lion.
They'd drag like Mithra in a week their burdens

down unholy trails and over mountains to the cave
that was Coruña. Exactly where the spears
of Charlemagne's unburied dead had sprouted leaves

along the Cea at the edge of Sahagún, they halted
their advance. By Alfonso's grave,
by the graves of Doña Berta & Constanza, his French queens,

by the ruins of the abbey that had rivaled Cluny
built by Jaca's Englishman
where Aimery Picaud had found unrivalled natural beauty

and a city radiant with grace,
these Englishmen of Sir John Moore's found news:
that Bonaparte himself had crossed the Duoro

and would crush them where they were or drive them
to the sea. They tumed and fled;
joined a procession of the living and the dead.

Before them, taurophorus, Mithra dragged the bull,
took its hooves upon his shoulders,
pulling it up mountain trails after Villafranca

in the sleet and snow. Behind them, in his death,
embalmed Rodrigo—tied to beams
that braced him in his saddle, dressed for combat,

sword in hand, looking like some exhumed agent
of the Holy Office driving
heretics to new trans-Cantabrian quemaderos....

...*tantas lanças premer e alçar,*
tanta adágara foradar e passar.... tanta loriga
falssar e desmanchar, tantos pendones

salir vermejos en sangre.... lances, bucklers,
coats of mail broken there,
pennons of the foreign legions soaked in blood...

If Suero de Quiñones read aloud the twenty-two
conditions of the tournament
in which he'd win his ransom at the Orbiego bridge

and then proclaim the Paso Honroso,
who would answer for these blood-shod infantry between
Bembibre and the Cua not *Oit Varones*...

but *Ahora sueña la razón?*
If reason drempt on this retreat, then so did song.
It slept and dreamed its monsters

in the language of a soldiery that spat and swore
cursing all the bridges
that would measure honor & had measured piety before.

No one shouted *Vivan los Ingleses* as they passed
through villages to loot & rape
where church bells rang when they had gone to summon Soult.

Stragglers broke into bodegas, smashed the wine casks,
then cut up the dying mules & bullocks
by the roadside that had pulled artillery & ammunition vans

to boil them in kettles on great fires they built with gun butts
and mix with what remained of issue brandy,
salted meats and biscuits and the buckets full of melted snow.

Those who dared to sleep were frozen dead by morning,
and when chasseurs came in twos & threes
to scout the strength of Moore's rear guard, they hacked

the arms off those who staggered in the wind
or split their heads down to their chins with sabers flashing
in the sun. All the rest was in the hills.

109

From Villafranca to Nogales, from
Nogales on through Lugo to Betanzos, darkness fell at noon,
the walls of houses cracked, down

from all the bell towers tumbled bells.
On the march, flames leapt from spears of ash & apple,
hauberks buckled, steel casques burst,

bears and leopards walked among the men
in John Moore's dream. For so he dreamed. Dreamed
within a dream his own high requiem before

the English ships sailed north from Vigo,
their mastheads and their prows decked and lighted
through the night with lamps and rubies

in the story that Trafalgar tells.
Miles, Corax, Heliodromus, Pater of the bas-reliefs,
he signed the zodiac of Mithra's solstice

and hallucinated Corybantes in the skins of beasts
and flagellants where General Paget
sought to make example of deserters and had lashed

at stunted icy trees men who'd
hidden in the windowless dark huts with sick & filthy
mountaineers and who, blinded by the days

of snow, could only hear what would accompany
their punishment: a jangling
of the manacles and fetters hanging on the branded

criminals who crawled the road before them
on their hands and knees and slept
with lepers under dark façades of abbeys, while

in Bonaparte's Madrid, El Sordo painted bulls.
Bulls and bodies of the slain—
dismembered and hung up on trees like ornaments:

arms and legs, heads with genitals stuffed
in their mouths, torsos
cut off at the waist and neck and shoulders.

These the *deformis formositas ac formosa deformitas*
of the hour—torsos and toros,
packed in ice, delivered down the trails to Picasso

in a year when internationals once more decamp in Spain....
Viva la Muerte's the Falangist song.
Lorca's murdered; Machado & Vallejo promptly die.

Trusting neither Mithra nor St. James, his eye
on anarchists in Barcelona,
Franco summons mercenary Moors to save the church.

VI

In the high places, they could hear the blast.
Ships rocked on the sea,
the houses at Coruña shook on their foundations

when the ammunition stores were blown.
At Santiago, bells that had burned Almanzor's oils
rang from the shock of it while men

whose job it was to ring them stood
amazed out in the square & wondered if this thunder
and the ringing was in time for Vespers

or for Nones or if it was entirely out of time.
The thunder and the ringing echoed
down the trails, back to San Millán, San Juan de la Peña,

while Maragatos looked up from their plows
and Basque shepherds among flocks near Roncevaux
turned their backs on the west & hunched

down under tall protective rocks jutting up
in frosty and transhumant fields.
Then in the high & highest places everything was still.

As it was in the beginning. Before Saint Francis
came down from the hills to Rocaforte,
before he taught his brothers how to preach & sing the word

to their little sister birds who flew into the tallest trees
and over cliffs in threefold
colored and adoring coats; before the Logos

or the Duende moved in Bertsulari singing ancient
fueros of the Basques; before Ignatius
hammered out his disciplines among the mountain rocks

breaking on the igneous of will the *ignis fatuus*
of valleys & the vagaries of love.
As it was in the beginning....

Long before *it is*
and ever shall be under overhanging
rocks at San Juan de la Peña...where they say, they *say*

the Grail came to rest and made a fortress
of the monastery there carved beneath a cliff-face roof
where dowsers conjured water out of rock

in Mithra's Visigothic cave & his tauroctonous priest
drove the killing sword, like Manolete,
in the shoulder of the bellowing great beast

to burst its heart & bleed the plants & herbs across
the mountainside that monks would one day
gather there, bleed the wheat they'd make into their bread.

Everything, everything was still. As it was in the beginning
long before the silence of the abbeys,
the silence of the abbots in their solitary prayer,

the silence of the brothers cutting hay & tending sheep
at San Millán of the Cowl,
the silent sacristan measuring and pouring oils—

the weavers and the tailors and the copyists at work,
Cellarius among his stores of wool and flax,
Hortulanus in his garden tending bees—silence broken only

as Hebdomadarius, finished with the cooking, rings a bell
and even old Gonzalo de Berceo looks up happily
from silent pages where his saint has walked the mountains

in the language of Castillian *juglares* which is not,
God knows, the language of the Latin clerks. *Andaba por*
    los montes,
por los fuertes lugares, por las cuestas enhiestas,

but silently, and all around him it was very very still.
As it was in the beginning before silence,
in the silence that preceded silence, in the stillness

before anything was still, when nothing
made a single sound and singularity was only nothing's
song unsinging...aphonia

before a whisper or a breath, aphasia
before injury,
aphelion of outcry without sun...

                          Long before *it is*
and ever shall be under overhanging
rocks at San Juan de la Peña, at San Millán of the Cowl,

at Loyola's Casa-Torre and the shepherds' huts
of Bertsulari in the Pyrenees
when no one spoke of *fueros* or *tristitia* or *spes,*

114

and there were neither rights nor hopes nor
sadnesses to speak of.
Then in the high and highest places everything was
    still.

As it was in the beginning. As it will be in the end.

                    •

Towards Pamplona, long long after all Navarre
was Spain, and after the end
of the Kingdom of Aragón, & after the end of the end,

I, John, walked with my wife Diana
down from the Somport Pass following the silence
that invited and received my song

        after Europe's latest referendum. In the city of
the *encierro* and the festival of San Fermín, we drank
red wines of the Ribera— Baja Montaña, Tierra
Estella— hosted by Delgado-Gomez, genius of that
place and guide Picaud. From university to citadel to
bull ring, from cathedral to the Plaza del Castillo and
along the high banks of the Arga, we walked and talked
about the road to Santiago, El Cid Campeador, Zuma-
lacárregui and Carlist wars. For he, Delgado-Gomez,
was a native of that place. He knew the way to San Juan
de la Peña, to Leyre and Olite and Sanguessa—and so
we followed him along the river valleys, into hills, and
over arid plains in the Bardenas. And after seven days
and seven nights remembering the likes of Sancho the
Wise and Sancho the Strong, the battle of Navas de
Tolosa and the chains of Miramamolín wrapped
around a coat of arms, the three of us, blest and besot-
ted, burned by the sun but refreshed by all the waters of
the mountain streams, the shade of many cloisters, and

the breezes of the vineyards of Mañeru, crossed the Puente la Reina ourselves, and walked that trail leading to the sea at Finisterre.

And, in the high & highest places, everything was still.

Notes

An East Anglian Diptych

This is very much a "poem of place" located in those parts of Cambridgeshire, Suffolk and Norfolk linked by the ley lines and rivers which connect locality with locality, and time with time. The ley lines in question are the ancient paths and tracks which date back to the neolithic period. The chief ley line followed is the Icknield Way, the track explored by Edward Thomas in his final volume of prose on the English countryside. Thomas himself figures in the prose section of the first part of the sequence, section iv. The controlling myth for both "Ley Lines" and "Rivers" derives from T.C. Lethbridge's *Gogmagog: The Buried Gods*, which treats the old Celtic/Belgic religion in terms of his excavation of the Wandelbury chalk figures and their relationship to better known hill figures such as the Cerne Giant. The presiding presences in "Ley Lines" (who also return in "Rivers") are the dowser—Lethbridge himself was a dowser—and his prototype, the Dodman, who was the prehistoric surveyor who aligned the paths and tracks. The transition between the "Ley Lines" section and the "Rivers" is made by way of the terrestrial zodiac at Bury St. Edmund's, a vast arrangement of figures by means of which I move from the Sagittarius beginning on the River Lark near Abbots Bridge in Bury to the Gemini (in the form of Wandil, the East Anglian devil) standing on the Stour near Clare Castle. The rivers dealt with are, in order, the Stour, the Alde, and the Deben. As in "Ley Lines," this section shuttles backwards and forwards in time, though its geographical or topological movement is direct enough. This part too has a section in prose, John Constable on the Stour corresponding to Edward Thomas on the Icknield Way. The gods and goddesses invoked in both sections are the same: Gog (the sun/Bel/Baal/Belenus/Helith, etc.), Magog (the moon/Meg/Magg/Epona, etc.), and Wandil (darkness/ the East Anglian devil/the giant with a sword, etc.). When the last section of "Ley Lines" moves into the present by counting off the numbers which locate Whittlesford church on the Ordnance Survey Map, the fit of alliteration is not gratuitous. The Shiela-na-gig figure over the Whittlesford church door is an image of Gogmagog, and Lethbridge argues that words like "goggle," "giggle," "ogle," and the child's grotesque toy "Golliwog" are all verbal derivations. The end of "Rivers," like the end of "Ley Lines," also moves into the present— but without the fit of alliteration.

Sources: T.C. Lethbridge, *GogMagog*; Shirley Toulson, *East Anglia: Walking the Ley Lines and Ancient Tracks*; W.G. Arnott, *Alde Estuary, Orwell Estuary: The Story of Ipswich River, Suffolk Estuary: The Story of the River Deben*; George Ewart Evans, *The Pattern Under the Plough, Ask the Fellows Who Cut the Hay*; Julia Pipe, *Port on the Alde*; R. Allen Brown, *Orford Castle*; F.J.E. Raby and P.K. Baillie Reynolds, *Framlingham Castle*; O.R. Sitwell, *Framlingham Guide*; Julian Tennyson, *Suffolk Scene*; Rupert Bruce-Mitford, *The Sutton Hoo Ship Burial*; Bernice Grohskopf, *The Treasure of Sutton Hoo*; Michael Alexander, trans., *Beowulf*; W.J. Ashley, ed., *Edward III and His Wars, 1327-1360*; Michael Prestwich, *The Three Edwards*; William Longman, *The Life and Times of Edward the Third*.

Facts From An Apocryphal Midwest

I have grappled in this poem with some midwestern American geography, geology, pre-history and history that parallel in many ways those I was working with in "An East Anglian Diptych." The chief trails this time— American ley lines, as it were— began as prehistoric paths down which Lake Superior copper was carried from the early days of the Mound Builders until the collapse of their particular economy and way of life. These trails, and especially the Old Sauk Trail and the St. Joseph-Kankakee portage, were later used by the Potawatomi, the Miami and other local Algonquian tribes, as well as by the Iroquois on their raids into the area, and by the French explorers, traders and missionaries. Again, as in the East Anglian poem, three rivers figure in the topographical configuration that emerges: the St. Joseph (which the French called the River of Miamis), the Kankakee (also called the Seignelay), and the Illinois. The dominant historical figure in the poem is Réné-Robert Cavelier, Sieur de La Salle. Having begun my research while still at work on "An East Anglian Diptych" and having determined to write about rivers and trails which I often crossed but as yet knew little about, I found myself stimulated by exactly those things which from time to time I had thought might stimulate "another poet" as I sat writing about things I knew and loved in East Anglia—La Salle's voyage through the great lakes and journey along the local paths and waterways, Algonquian (mostly Potawatomi) history and mythology, the geological and geographical transformations which occurred during the last glacial recession, and the prose of Francis Parkman in the volume of *France and England in North America* called *La Salle and the Discovery of the Great West.* What had begun as an act of will rapidly became, in the actual processes of composition, altogether something else. Although I do not take La Salle all the way to the Mississippi (usually called the Colbert in the poem), I take him pretty far down the Illinois. For some of the same reasons that Edward Thomas and John Constable appear in "An East Anglian Diptych," Parkman himself appears briefly here. His prose is sometimes quoted, paraphrased, versified. Where quotations are not exact, I intend no disrespect. Formal constraints now and then demanded slight modifications in rhythm, diction and syntax. Neither Fenimore Cooper's stagecoach ride into the area nor the dedication of the cornerstone of the La Salle Memorial Project are fictions. The merging of the two, however, in the context of a pageant which occurred at the quatro-millennial anniversary of the La Salle-Miami Council is only a convenient way, consistent with the conclusions of both "Ley Lines" and "Rivers" in "An East Anglian Diptych," to bring the poem into the present historical period.

Among the sources for this poem are three that very few readers will have come across. These are books by an almost vanished breed, the local amateur historian. Charles H. Bartlett's *La Salle in the Valley of the St. Joseph*, George A. Baker's *The St. Joseph-Kankakee Portage*, and Timothy Edward Howard's *A History of St. Joseph County* were all enormously useful. Other sources for the poem include: Charles Haight Farnham, *A Life of Francis Parkman*; Howard Doughty, *Francis Parkman*; Louise Phelps Kellogg, *Early Narratives of the Northwest* and *The French Regime in Wisconsin and the Northwest*; Henri Joutel, *A Journal of La Salle's Last Voyage*; Carl O. Sauer, *Seventeenth Century North America* and *Selected Essays 1963-1975*; James A. Clifton, *The Prairie People*; R. David Edmunds, *The Potawatomis*; George T. Hunt, *The*

Wars of the Iroquois; Fay Folsom Nichols, *The Kankakee*;
Archer Butler Hulbert, *Indian Thoroughfares*; Hugh
Brody, *Maps and Dreams*; Andrew Trout, *Jean-Baptiste
Colbert*; James Fenimore Cooper, *The Oak Openings: or
The Bee Hunter*; George Dekker, *James Fenimore Cooper:
The American Scott*; Blake Nevius, *Cooper's Landscapes:
An Essay on the Picturesque Vision*. The dedication of this
poem reflects formal debts as well as friendship. "An
East Anglian Diptych" began as a homage to David
Jones and Robert Duncan. The present poem, begin-
ning with its title, takes a leaf from Ken Smith's *The Poet
Reclining* and some strategies from Michael Anania's
The Color of Dust and *Riversongs*.

A Compostela Diptych

The final poem in what, from the summer of 1984 to
the winter of 1990, slowly took the form of a trilogy,
deals with the most distinguished trails of them all: the
pilgrimage routes to Santiago de Compostela. Having
written two poems where I felt on very familiar
ground— though in two different ways— I began in
1986 to meditate a poem about a ground with which I
was totally unfamiliar, except through the literature to
which it had given birth from the troubadours to Wal-
ter Starkie and Eleanor Munro. In the summer of 1987
I walked parts of the Via Tolosana over Somport Pass
and on through Jaca, San Juan de la Peña, Leyre, San-
guesa, Pamplona, Puente la Reina, Estella, Logroño,
Nájera, Santo Domingo de la Calzada, and Burgos,
crossing back into France through the pass at Ronces-
valles. I did not reach Santiago itself, and I do not reach
Santiago in the poem. The writing, however, became a
pilgrimage in earnest when, without warning, I had

121

first to help another person struggle towards physical and spiritual health, and then, unwell myself, begin a similar journey of my own.

As with the two earlier poems in the trilogy, I have more debts than I can possibly acknowledge. Stylistically, David Jones is once again a welcome and benevolent presence. Indeed his good help and hope have actually become, in a sense, one of the subjects of the present poem. The same could be said of Ezra Pound up through the walk from Excidieul. I have leaned heavily on a number of translations. Although the poet knows the various languages which he must sometimes quote all too imperfectly himself, the poem's polylingual texture is essential: it is necessary for the reader to try and hear the Latin, French, Spanish and Provençal words as best he can. I need particularly to acknowledge W.S. Merwin's translation of the *Poema del Cid*, Robert Harrison's and Dorothy L. Sayers' translations of the *Chanson de Roland*, and the three translations, one into French and two into English, of the Pilgrim's Guide attributed to Aimery Picaud from the *Codex Calixtinus* listed below with my full range of sources. Walter Starkie's *The Road to Santiago*, Roman Menéndez Pidal's *The Cid and His Spain*, and Eleanor Munro's *On Glory Roads* have been my constant companions. (Much in Part I derives from Munro's interpretation of the visual setting and internal structures of pilgrimage in the light of archaeo- and ethno-astronomical theory.) Occasional phrases from these books turn up in the poem itself, as also from the texts by Meyer Shapiro, Erwin Panofsky, Umberto Eco, Jules Michelet, Thomas Carlyle, Desmond Seward, Jacques Lacarriere, Emmanuel Le Roy Ladurie, Henry Chadwick, Alphonsus M. Liguori, Edward Peters, John James, Jan Read, J.A. Condé, Oleg Grabar, Henry Kamen, Christopher

122

Hibbert, Franz Cumont, Henry Sedgwick, Johan Huizinga, Bruno S. James, Edgar Holt and Adam Nicholson listed below. Borrowings in the poem are usually indicated by italics.

Sources for Part I: Jeanne Vielliard, *Guide De Pèlerin de Saint-Jacques de Compostelle* (Texte Latin du XIIe Siècle, Édité et Traduit en Francais d'Après Les Manuscripts de Compostelle et de Ripoll); Constantine Christofides, *Notes Toward a History of Medieval and Renaissance Art, with a Translation of 'The Pilgrim's Guide to Saint-James of Compostela'*; Paula L. Gerson, Annie Shaver-Crandall, & M. Alison Stones, eds. & translators, *Pilgrims' Guide to Santiago de Compostela*; A. Kingsley Porter, *Romanesque Sculpture of the Pilgrimage Roads*; Meyer Shapiro, *Romanesque Art*; Joseph Gantner, *The Glory of Romanesque Art*; Vera Hell, *The Great Pilgrimage of the Middle Ages*; Eusebio Goicoechea Arrondo, *The Way to Santiago; El Camino de Santiago: Guia Del Peregrino*; Eleanor Munro, *On Glory Roads: A Pilgrim's Book about Pilgrimage*; Walter Starkie, *The Road to Santiago*; Noreen Hunt, *Cluniac Monasticism in the Central Middle Ages, Cluny Under Saint Hugh 1049-1109*; Jacobus de Voragine, *The Golden Legend* (translated and adapted from the Latin by Granger Ryan and Helmut Ripperger); Christopher Page, *Voices and Instruments of the Middle Ages: Instrumental Practice and Songs in France 1100-1300*; Russell Chamberlin, *The Emperor Charlemagne*; Charles Edward Russell, *Charlemagne: First of the Moderns*; Peter Munz, *Life in the Age of Charlemagne*; H.R. Loyn and John Percival, *The Reign of Charlemagne: Documents on Carolingian Government and Administration*; H.W. Garrod and R.B. Mowat, eds, *Einhard's Life of Charlemagne*; Robert Harrison, trans., *The Song of Roland*; Dorothy L. Sayers, trans., *The Song of Roland*; Edward Peters, *Heresy and Authority in Medieval Europe*;

Msgr. Leon Cristiani, *Heresies and Heretics*; St. Alphonsus M. Liguori, *The History of Heresies, and their refutation* (trans. from the Italian by the Rev. John T. Mullock); Henry Chadwick, *Priscillian of Avila*; Jacques Lacarriere, *The Gnostics*; Emmanuel Le Roy Ladurie, *Montaillou: The Promised Land of Error*; Joseph R. Strayer, *The Albigensian Crusades*; Desmond Seward, *Eleanor of Aquitaine: The Mother Queen*; Johan Huizinga, *The Waning of the Middle Ages*; Peter Makin, *Provence and Pound*; Adam Nicholson, *Long Walks in France*. Sources for "Intercalation": Erwin Panofsky, ed. and trans., *Abbot Suger on the Abbey Church of St.-Denis and Its Art Treasures*; Umberto Eco, *Art and Beauty in the Middle Ages*; Bruno S. James, *Saint Bernard of Clairvaux*; Donald Francis Firebaugh, *St. Bernard's Preaching of the Second Crusade*; Thomas Merton, *The Last of the Fathers*; Henry Adams, *Mont-Saint-Michel and Chartres*; Steven Runciman, *A History of the Crusades*; Odo of Deuil, *De Profectione Ludovici Vll in Orientem*; John Hugh Hill and Laurita Lyttleton Hill, *Raymond IV Count of Toulouse*; Jules Michelet, *History of the French Revolution*, Vol. VII (Books 14,15,16 and 17), trans. by Keith Botsford; Thomas Carlyle, *The French Revolution*; John James, *The Traveller's Key to Medieval France: A Guide to the Sacred Architecture of Medieval France*. Sources for Part II: J.A. Condé, *History of the Dominion of the Arabs in Spain*; Jan Read, *The Moors in Spain and Portugal*; Oleg Grabar, *The Formation of Islamic Art*; Keith Albarn, Jenny Miall Smith, Stanford Steele, Diana Walker, *The Language of Pattern*; W.S. Merwin, trans, *The Poem of the Cid* (with facing page Spanish text of the edition of Ramon Menéndez Pidal), *From the Spanish Morning: Translations of Spanish Ballads*; Ramon Menéndez Pidal, *The Cid and His Spain, Poesia Juglaresca y Origenes de las Literaturas Romancias*; Ernest Merimée and S. Griswold Morley, *A History of Spanish Literature*; David William

Foster, *The Early Spanish Ballad*; Cecil Roth, *The Spanish Inquisition*; Henry Kamen, *The Spanish Inquisition*; David Gates, *The Spanish Ulcer: A History of the Peninsular War*; Richard Humble, *Napoleon's Peninsular Marshals*; Christopher Hibbert, *Corunna*; W.H. Fitchett, ed., *Wellington's Men: Some Soldier Autobiographies*; C.S. Forester, *The Gun*; Hugh Thomas, *The Spanish Civil War*; Franz Cumont, *The Mysteries of Mithra*; M.J. Vermaseren, *Mithras: The Secret God*; Francisco Goya, *The Complete Etchings, Aquatints and Lithographs*; Eleanor Elsner, *The Romance of the Basque Country and the Pyrenees*; Johannes Jorgensen, *St. Francis of Assisi*; Omer Englebert, *Saint Francis of Assisi*; Henry Dwight Sedgwick, *Ignatius Loyola*; Mary Purcell, *The First Jesuit*; Walter Nigg, *Warriors of God: The Great Religious Orders and their Founders*; W.S. Porter, *Early Spanish Monasticism*; Edgar Holt, *The Carlist Wars in Spain*.

A Note about the Author

A native of Ohio, John Matthias teaches English at the University of Notre Dame. He has been Visiting Fellow in Poetry at Clare Hall, Cambridge, and lived for much of the 1970s in the East Anglia region of England. He has published four previous volumes of poetry with Swallow Press: *Bucyrus* (1971), *Turns* (1975), *Crossing* (1979), and *Northern Summer: New and Selected Poems* (1984). *Bathory & Lermontov* (1980) and *Två Dikter* (1989) were published in Sweden. With Göran Printz-Påhlson, he edited and translated *Contemporary Swedish Poetry* (Swallow, 1980) and with Vladeta Vučković he translated *The Battle of Kosovo* (Swallow, 1987). His own work has been translated into Swedish, Dutch, French, German, Greek, and Serbo-Croat. He has edited *23 Modern British Poets* (Swallow, 1971), *Introducing David Jones* (Faber and Faber, 1980), and *David Jones: Man and Poet* (The National Poetry Foundation, 1989). John Matthias has won numerous awards for his poetry and translations, most recently an Ingram Merrill Foundation grant for 1990.